Sailors, Waterways and Tugboats I have known

The New York State Barge Canal System

Sailors, Waterways and Tugboats I have known

The New York State Barge Canal System

Capt. Fred G. Godfrey

Library Research Associates Inc.
Monroe, New York
1993

Maps and background information have been provided by the
following:
James Pel Principe, Business Administration Bureau, Albany,NY
Columbia Encyclopedia (3rd edition, 1963)

Library Research Associates Inc.
Dunderberg Road, RD#5-Box 41
Monroe, New York 10950-3703

Library of Congress Cataloging-in-Publication Data

Godfrey, Fred G., 1915-
    Sailors, Waterways and Tugboats I have known by Fred
G. Godfrey.
    142p.
    Includes photos, maps, index.
    ISBN:0-912526-61-0
    1. Seafaring life -- New York (State) -- New York State
Barge Canal System. 2. Godfrey, Fred G., 1915-   -- Journeys.
3. Tugboats -- New York (State) -- New York State Barge Canal
System. I. Title
G540.G47   1993
386'.48'09747 -- dc20   92-42484
                                                              CIP

Dedication:

To my beloved daugther,

Patricia

Relaxing with a book.

Table of Contents

Author's sister Marion

Apparatus for steering when 2 or more barges are coupled together.

Preface

I have always had a great love for tugboats and my life has been closely intertwined with them. My father, a boy in a canalboat family, went to work for himself as soon as he was big enough. He operated a pair of lumber boats for Griffin Lumber Company (Hudson Falls, N.Y.) and later went to other barges, some of which he may have owned.

Griffin Lumber Co. of Hudson Falls, N.Y.

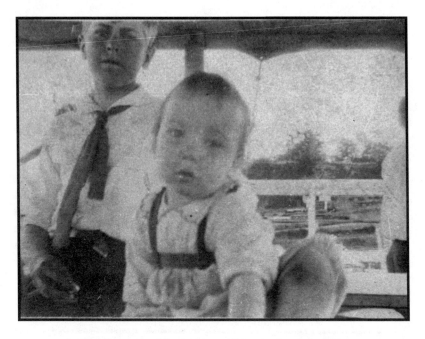

**Author harnessed for safety and uncle, Reginald Ross
Glens Falls, N.Y.**

My parents were operating a barge canal boat in 1915, when my mother went ashore to visit her mother in Glens Falls and to give birth. When Mother had regained her strength after I was born, we returned to the boat. I recollect only stories that my parents told me. No doubt I saw tugs at that time and became attracted to them. We left the boats before I became of school age and my father went to work on tugboats.

A favorite toy, a few years later, was made by sawing a point on a short length of board, driving a nail near the point, and tying a string to the nail. This became my toy tugboat and was preferred to other toys that were purchased.

At age ten, I taught my friends the bell system used on the tugs. We would take turns riding or pushing my coaster wagon, being guided ahead or astern by the pretended ringing of such bells. Most boys in my block soon learned the bell system.

The early steamboat days are remembered by me with great pleasure.

**Author's mother posing with the spring pole on the tin pump.
Note tiller and also frame to support awning.**

Western End of the Great Erie Canal at Buffalo (about 1830).
Buffalo Historical Society

Introduction

When completed, the New York State Barge Canal System was 525 miles long, traversing New York State and connecting the Great Lakes with the Hudson River and Lake Champlain. The Barge Canal was a modification and improvement of the old Erie Canal, approved in 1903 by a public vote. Construction began in 1905 and was completed in 1918.

Major sections are the Erie Canal which extends from Troy to Tonawanda; the Champlain Canal that joins the Erie Canal at Waterford and extends (via the Hudson River as far as Fort Edward) to Whitehall on Lake Champlain; the Oswego Canal that connects the Erie Canal with Oswego on Lake Ontario; and the Cayuga and Seneca Canal that joins the Erie Canal with Cayuga and Seneca Lakes.

The twelve-foot-deep Barge Canal has 310-foot electrically operated locks and accommodates 2,000-ton vessels. It cost New York State more than $175,000,000 to build, but was toll free.

The passage of eighty-five years has brought many changes to the New York State Barge Canal System. Marine technology eliminated steam-powered tugs and the development of air and highway transportation lessened the use of the tugs and barges. But a new use has grown from the tourist trade that now enjoys pleasure cruises on the scenic and historic Canals.

M.A.G.
January 1993

The Erie Canal is one of the most popular routes to the West. Passage from Albany to Buffalo, 364 miles, costs about $5.50 to $7.50 on most boats. Shown here is one of the locks, at Lockport, N.Y. Water is pumped into the lock to lift boats going west to higher elevations. Going east, water is let out of the lock to float the boats down.

Chapter 1

The first tugboat trip I made was aboard the *Triton*, although I do not remember it. My dad was captain of the single crew tug and he took me for a ride. The vessel was tied up for the night and, as I was only four years old, I was asleep in Dad's bunk in the pilot house. A fire broke out and father gathered me up in the blankets and laid me on the dock. The fire was extinguished and I was returned to the bed, still asleep, unaware of the excitement.

Some years later I was deckhand-cook on the *Triton*. As a deckhand I was fine, as a cook I was barely adequate. The skipper said I was a successful cook because I didn't get behind in the "grub money" and didn't lose a man. He was right. The grub money was $.90 per man per day. For this four man crew $3.60 had to buy all food plus ice for refrigeration.

The *Triton*, like other Erie canal tugs of the time, carried a water barrel on the bow deck which provided all water used for drinking and cooking. Often a chunk of sulpher was placed in the bottom of the barrel to keep the water pure, but I never thought it helped. All other water used was dipped from the canal or the river. Steamboats with a fresh water tank in the bow for the boiler had a pitcher pump in the galley. *Triton* had no water tank and no pump. In good weather the crewmen would dip a pail of water from alongside the tug, heat it with steam from the boiler and do their washing, shaving or whatever on the side deck where the rail was a convenient place to set the pail. There was no shortage of water (though it might be a little brown in the canal) and it could be heated in about 5 seconds. A soap dish made from a tin can would be fastened under the rail. What more could you ask for?

Cooking on these old steamboats was done on a black coal-burning range, usually a Shipmate. Fueled by the same soft coal used to feed the boiler, but some boats had hard coal for the galley. On a day boat, the fire was allowed to die out at night.

In the morning, I would take a deck pail to the fireroom, fill it with hot coals, and run with it to the galley range, where I would turn on the jet in the smokestack for draft and get an instant fire. It was hot work and more than a little smokey.

Triton **was built at Buffalo, N.Y. in 1899**

The galley on the *Triton* was below deck in the bow and the only ventilation was the companionway to enter it. The ship's boiler, with all its heat, was directly behind the galley's after bulkhead. Cooking on the cast iron range created a temperature like Hades. Crew members usually filled a plate and ate on deck, but the deckhand was down there for the cooking, dishwashing and cleaning as well as running up the stairway to coal up, haul ashes, handle lines, clean ship, and perhaps to relieve the captain at the wheel. For this, he received $70 for a month of twelve hour days, but there was no shortage of applicants for the job.

The *Triton* was nearing the end of her career, but the owners decided to spend some dollars on her with a new high pilot house which the skipper appreciated. The toilet facility was still a small closet with a pail setting on the deck and a toilet seat hinged on the bulkhead so as to swing down over the pail. The pail was dumped overboard, rinsed, and returned for the next use. Unfortunately, the old wooden hull was deteriorating and the carpenters trying to refasten a hull plank in the side above the water line, found a rib so rotted they could not fasten a spike in it.

"Pickerel Pete" Matte, engineer and son John Matte, fireman.
About 1937.

They bored a hole through and installed a bolt from the outer to the inner planks to hold them in place then smeared it with grease and coal dust to hide it. The lower engine room was so dark that the inspectors never noticed. The tugboatmen knew it but did not care, as the *Triton* never went out of the canal and they felt in no danger. A year or so later the Steamboat Inspectors said the first plank on each side of the keel must be removed for inspection of the hull. Everyone knew this was a death blow so she was scrapped. Thus ended the *Triton*, God of the Sea!

Captain George Godfrey at Lock #8 Schenectady

Chapter 2

My father was captain of the *George Field* in 1925. This fine little tug, built at Buffalo, N.Y. in 1882, was based in Waterford and did local work as a day boat with a three-man crew. She towed brick scows from area brickyards such as Crescent and Mechanicville, brought sand out of Vischer's Ferry, Searles Ferry, Wilbur's Basin, and Mechanicville, and did other towing. She had a low pilot house, that was later raised to the upper deck and a galley installed beneath it.

Bill Bogert, the engineer-fireman, was like a second father to me. I liked the bright gold tooth that showed every time he grinned, which was often. When running light, I used to sneak into the engine room and edge the throttle open a little more so we would go faster. After a few such trips the engine would be running at maximum speed. Bill surely knew what was going on, but he let me believe that I was getting away with something. The little tug could only make about ten knots.

George TenEyck was my father's deckhand and a close personal friend of many years. George would show me how to coil decklines and let me shovel coal off the deck. At the end of the day, I would be very dirty and my grandmother would express strong disapproval when I got home. Then I would get the standard lecture that if I grew up and went to work on the boats she would disown me. (I did and she didn't.)

I spent much of my summer vacation aboard this ship and enjoyed it immensely. My dad had a wooden box in the pilot house for me to stand on so I could see out of the windows while he taught me to steer. He taught me how to run the buoys and which places to beware of. Tugs were all "cross gear" at that time so I had to learn to turn the wheel to starboard if I wanted the tug to go to port, and vice versa. About 1936 a law was enacted which compelled all steamboats to have direct steering. At that time we returned to the more natural method, but the steering lessons I received from my father came in very handy a short time later.

In the summer of 1927, I was almost 12 years old. My friend Hugh Cameron, Jr., of Fort Edward was visiting me and we went for a day trip on the tug which at this time operated as a "dinner pail boat." This meant there was no cooking done and the crew carried their food with them. Hugh and I went aboard. The tug was tied up at, what was then, the end of the Waterford Terminal wall by the old cider mill. Across the street was Castracani's store where boatmen could get groceries, ice, kerosene, and other supplies, including what came out of the back room to quench their thirsts. The entire crew went there to get some sandwiches made and they returned after a while with some food, but then decided to make another visit to the back room. When they returned sometime later, they were far from sober.

The lines were cast off and the light tug taken over to the old malt house at 120th Street, Lansingburg. Two light scows were picked up on the short stern lines and we were headed for the paper mill at Mechanicville. My father turned the wheel over to the deckhand and went to bed in the bunkroom on the main deck aft.

Our regular deckhand was a licensed pilot, lent to John E. Matton & Co. to captain a tug for a short time. We had one of Matton's deckhands temporarily, a new man I did not know, who headed the tug and tow up the Hudson. Hugh and I were uncomfortable with all these proceedings. As we approached the Waterford bridge the tug was heading toward the abutment. I was frightened and told the deckhand that he was going to hit it. His reply was,

"I work for Matton not Murray, and I'm going to sink this old banner."

I gave him a shove and he collapsed on the deck. I hurriedly muscled the big wheel over to avoid hitting the bridge. The tug and tow were now in my care and I was a scared kid.

My friend Hugh, at my frantic urging, tried to awaken my father but did not succeed. I saw Bill, the engineer, hanging over the rail emptying his stomach and I called to him to get my father up. Bill just laughed and said,

"Buster, you're doing fine."

Capt. Clayton H. Godfrey and crew of *Fannie L. Baker*, owned by John E. Matton, with oil barge alongside. This captain, with this tug is said to be the first to push an oil barge in the canal by lashing the tug to it with steel cables.

There never was a more frightened pilot and passenger than we two boys. I steered the tug and tow up the river, through Lock #1, and into Lock #2, still unable to get my father up. The locktenders gave us some puzzled looks but probably thought my father was in the galley or another part of the boat. I worried about the fast water below Lock #3 and I was terrified to think about going along the top of the dam above the lock. Lucky for me, I was able to rouse my father in Lock #2 and he took over. What a relief! Bill said that I had done a fine job. Dad complimented me and slipped me a fifty cent piece with the admonition,

"Don't tell your grandmother."

I never did.

The one fault I found with this ship was the lack of toilet facilities, there was no head. The crew, when necessary, used a shovel full of coal in the fireroom and then threw it into the firebox. The fireroom was the one place I would not enter, so I waited until evening tie up and went ashore. Other than this, in my boyhood memories the *George Field* is one of my favorite tugboats.

Chapter 3

Arriving at St. Jean, P.Q., Canada with tow in 1932

The *Junior Murray*, (built at New Baltimore, N.Y. in 1909) formerly the *Edna J. Brooks*, was a workboat past her prime when I knew her but she was dependable, economical on coal, and always seemed to have a happy crew.

Her water-logged wooden hull was heavy and her depth was 10′ plus, so one had to be careful in shallow parts of the canal. When running light, she would start "smelling bottom" and become hard to control with the old hand gear. She could not go down the Richelieu River into Canada during the low water months of midsummer because of her draft. When full of coal and fresh water the guardrail aft was in the water. The hull inspector insisted on draft marks on the stern, so an eleven-foot-mark was painted on her waist. If the water level ever reached that mark, she was sunk.

At one time, the *Junior* was towing an oil barge from Bayonne, N.J. to ports on the Erie Canal. She had very little freeboard. Leaving New York with fresh water tanks topped off and coal bunkers full, plus a deck load of coal, she was a real "rubber boot boat." The deck plates were kept on and the lower half doors on the engine room and fire room were kept closed because the deck was awash with every swell from passing vessels. It was instant relief when enough coal and water had been consumed so that the freeboard increased a couple of inches.

In the summer of 1932, during my school vacation, I returned to Troy after 5 years away from tugboats. The *Junior Murray* was operating as a four-man single-crew job. Most of her work consisted of taking second lockings through "The Flight" at Waterford. The deckhand-cook was Leon Fish from Champlain, N.Y., a licensed pilot who, like other pilots during these hard times, was working as a deckhand while waiting for conditions to improve. I went "hamming" aboard this ship for a couple of weeks, working as a deckhand to learn the trade and my pay was the food I ate — possibly ham. I learned the proper way to handle lines, etc., but refused to cook. Leon liked it because he could lie in his bunk at night and draw overtime pay while I did his work.

1932 - Note barge load of hay waiting to go south in tow.

There were some tricks to flight work which I learned at this time.

1 - Never touch the "jingle" bell for full ahead except in an emergency. Operation on "one bell" ahead produced almost the same speed and gave the fireman a better chance to regulate the steam pressure in the boiler.

2 - Never be caught just above Lock #2 when Lock #3 was dumped. The old Champlain Canal crossed the new Barge Canal at this point and when the water dumped from Lock #3 ran in and out of this area it was hard to control a tow.

3 - Don't be caught under a bridge by a back swell from the lock or you might lose your pilot house. (This was before the bridges were raised to twenty feet.)

4 - When entering a lock with a tow, the tug's bow should be placed against the miter sill on the starboard side and the stern should be swung against the opposite wall. The tug's stern should be between the lock wall and the bow of the head boat. This allows room for barges and tugs to lock together.

Once in a while the barge captain would stop the tow before it was fully in the lock and the locktender would not be able to close the gates. It was not necessary to pull the tow farther into the lock. One merely left the rudder hard right and worked the engine ahead. The action of the water would pull the tow the rest of the way into the lock.

This period of "hamming" taught me basic skills and gave me the opportunity to meet other boatmen. Because of this, I managed to pick up a few days temporary work here and there on the other tugs. As autumn approached, business picked up as it always did, so I wanted to stay and work, but my father shipped me back to school.

In June, 1933, after my high school graduation, I returned to Troy looking for a job. Capt. "Mike" LaFountain of Whitehall was master of *Junior Murray* and he needed a deckhand. I arrived at the opportune time and was hired.

The fireman was Leo Hurtibus of Whitehall. We became good friends as well as shipmates. The engineer was Bob Quick whose motto was "Quick by name and Quick by nature." I can't say enough good things about Bob. He was a good engineer, a hard worker, always cheerful, full of practical jokes, immaculately clean, and always ready to help his shipmates. He took me in hand for training and I soon found out how little I knew about being a good deckhand. He taught me how to cook, which made it a lot better for the crew. He rode me unmercifully about keeping the ship clean — particularly the galley and the crew's quarters. If my dungarees and shirt were not as clean as he thought they should be, I was told to clean up. A hole in my clothing was an invitation to him to insert a finger and rip the hole larger so the garment became unwearable. His comment was,

"Patch the hole or get new clothes." He was a demanding instructor, but I am glad he took an interest in me.

Bob washed his shirts and dungarees in a metal wash tub on the side deck. The clothes were covered with hot water and soap powder and allowed to soak. A hand plunger was left in the tub and used to wash the clothes as time permitted. Bad stains would be removed with a scrub brush and yellow soap. I dropped my dirty dungarees into the tub without his knowledge and they were washed for me. The second time I was told to do my own laundry. The third time I found that a couple of cans of lye had been added to the water after Bob's clothes were removed. The only usable parts of my dungarees left were the metal buttons.

As in the previous year, we were doing second lockings through "The Flight" for other companies. Sometimes we would work around the clock. In order to get some rest, the engineer and fireman would take turns running the engine and keeping up steam while the other man slept. Capt. Mike told me we would take turns steering the tug through the locks when we had no tow. this was fine for him, but it seemed that whenever it was my turn to sleep I had to wash dishes, or peel potatoes, or get breakfast, or some other chore. I would get so sleepy that when we had a tow I would lie across three galley stools and sleep the few minutes between locks. Fortunately, I always woke up when the engine stopped and I would dash for the stern deck to care for the stern lines.

It was desirable to wash the ship's boiler once a month, but it usually ran a couple weeks longer. This meant blowing off steam, cooling the boiler down, punching soot out of the boiler tubes, washing silt and sediment out of the boiler, refilling it, and getting up steam again. Twenty four hours was the normal time allowed for this.

One Saturday night, we were running light down "The Flight" bound for 120th Street to tie up and wash boiler. Bob, the engineer, decided it would be too late in the evening to fully celebrate Saturday night if he waited until we tied up to blow down the boiler. The fireman was told to pull his fires leaving Lock #3, which he did. Entering Lock #2, I threw a bow line over a post on the wall and snubbed the tug to a stop so that the engine would not have to be reversed, thus saving some steam. The operator gave us a rather slow locking and we were wondering if we had enough steam left to make it across the river. The propeller was barely flopping over when we reached the dock. We would have appeared to be very stupid if we had not made it to the dock. The engine room boys thus had some extra time to spend at Harold Roberts' place, formerly Bob Roberts' speakeasy.

Another Saturday night, we were returning from Searles Ferry with a barge loaded with sand (possibly the last boatload ever shipped from there). The end of the work day found us at Lock #1. The barge was tied up below the lock. Mike asked us if we wanted to go to 120th Street and, of course, we all thought it a great idea. We left the barge and headed south. It was dark but I was told not to light the running lights as the captain did not want anyone to see us going down the river. This was all right with me as we had no electricity and I did not want to dirty the kerosene lamps. We ghosted down the river and quietly slipped in alongside the *Triton*, which was tied up there. A voice out of the darkness asked, "What are you doing here?" It was my father, who was marine superintendent of the company. He had watched us stealing down the river and was on the *Triton*, standing in the dark, ready to surprise us with a greeting when we arrived. We thought we were in trouble, but all turned out well. Dad knew about the monotony of a seven day work week of twelve hour days with no recreation. He warned us to be careful and left. We then had our Saturday night celebration.

Business picked up as it usually did in the fall. The *Junior* was double crewed and put to work in the western canal. Leo Hurtibus held a license so he was promoted to assistant engineer. Charlie Austin of Whitehall, and another man whose name I have forgotten, were hired as firemen. Maurice Vermet of Whitehall became the deckhand, Harry Young the mate, and Israel La White of Whitehall the cook.

Harry, the new mate, suggested that I ask the captain for permission to go on the second watch (12 to 6 morning and night). He explained that, being autumn, we would have much fog between midnight and morning so the tow would be tied up, and we could sleep rather than be working. That sounded good to me. Captain Mike gave me permission, thus he got a more experienced deckhand on his watch. Harry was right about the fog, but not my sleep. The tow was usually shoved on the bank when in fog and the crew went to sleep except for me. I was delegated to stand watch.

The sleeping quarters were very tight for a double crew. The captain and mate were okay in the after part of the pilot house. The other seven were packed into one small room on the main deck aft. There were three bunks against the after bulkhead for the engineers and cook. Four bunks against the forward bulkhead were for the firemen and deckhands. There was room for only one man at a time to dress or undress. A single chair sat between the two tiers of bunks. Above the chair, a short length of pipe was hung from the overhead. Each man was allowed one coathanger for any dress clothes he had. A blue bed sheet was wrapped around the seven hangers to keep the clothes clean. All work clothing or other apparel was kept under one's mattress. No dirty clothes were permitted, so every time a change was made, the dirty clothes were washed immediately, dried and put away.

Bob Quick again laid down the law about cleanliness in the crew's quarters, and he enforced it. The deckhands and firemen were to take turns in cleaning the room every day between 5:30 and 6:00 a.m. No excuse for non-performance would be accepted.

Maurice was a good deckhand, an outdoorsman (hunter, trapper, fisherman), strong as a bull, with a good disposition, and clean and neat. He and I got along well together. We decided that the cramped space between the bunks was not enough so we went to the hot bed system. The top bunk was removed and the next bunk was used turn-in and turn out every six hours. The bed sheets never got cool. There now was a lot of room above our bunk, especially as it was up in the skylight. We installed a shelf to hold our shaving gear, cigarettes, and other personal effects, and were quite comfortable. I would not want to use this system with some other shipmates I have had.

Some adjustments had to be made when changing from single crew to double crew operation. The first crew worked 6 to 12 morning and evening and the second watch worked from 12 to 6. The tug ran 24 hours a day with the usual noises that accompanied this operation. These might include the sound of whistles blowing, bells ringing, clanging of tools dropped on the steel deck in the fire room, or the banging of the ash bucket on the rail when hauling ashes. The noise of coal being dumped on deck and into the bunkers was annoying as was the consequent listing of the tug as each side bunker was filled in its turn. A new man had great difficulty sleeping. He would be unable to sleep for 24 hours, but then tired out and accustomed to the noise, he would sleep soundly. The slow turning of the old steam engines sent a rhythmic beat through the hull and gave a pleasant sensation for sleeping — like a baby rocked in a cradle. Many crewmen would awake immediately when the engine stopped.

The *Junior Murray* had no electricity, and Harry Young came aboard with a long five cell flashlight. The pilot house men were greatly disadvantaged operating at night with no searchlight. (A generator, electric lights, and a searchlight were installed the following year.)

It was my job to clean and fill the lanterns each day. Cook would not allow me to do this in the galley, so to get out of the cold and bad weather, I would sit on top of the asbestos covered boiler while doing this chore. Bob Quick started calling me "Asbestos." My feelings were hurt because I thought he was referring to the position at which I worked best. All was well when he said he meant that I must have asbestos pants to sit on the hot boiler.

That autumn was a very happy cruise time for me. I was getting paid while seeing many new sights, such as the Erie Canal with the high Lock #17 at Little Falls, the double lock at Lockport, Oneida Lake, the Oswego Canal to Oswego, the Niagara River, and Buffalo harbor. My knowledge was further increased when, passing Tonawanda bound for Buffalo, we went by a street of little frame buildings. Several girls came out and waved to us and gestured to their house. I was told that this was known as Goose Island and the girls were prostitutes.

N.Y.S.D.P.W. tug *National* at Brewerton, N.Y. This tug once stood watch at Brewerton as rescue ship for vessels in trouble on Onieda Lake. Note weather tower. Another tower was at Sylvan Beach. Vessels could get latest weather from them.

On the last trip of the season, we had coaled up at Rome and were headed east with a tow. It was a bitter cold and dark morning (5:00 a.m.) with ice forming on the water as I stood in the pilot house with the mate. When we were approaching Rome Guard Gate, I left to go to the stern and to stand by the hawsers.

Billy Murray and **Junior Murray**
after delivering a tow to St. Jean, P.Q. in 1937.

I came down the ladder from the upper deck face forward instead of the safer way of backing down. We had a deck load of coal and I stepped on a piece of coal, lost my balance, and unable to recover, jumped to get clear of the tug. The cold water momentarily knocked the wind out of me. When I recovered my breath, I began shouting. Because of the cold, everything aboard ship was closed up tight and no one heard me. The tug and tow were moving slowly, but I had so many watersoaked clothes on that I had difficulty swimming. Finally, the mate heard me and rang the engine down to dead slow. He could not stop nor leave the wheel as we were almost in the guard gate. I swam to the tug and grabbed the guard rail near the stern quarter bitts. My heavy clothes would not permit me to reach up any higher, nor to pull myself farther forward on the tug. My feet were being pulled in towards the propeller. I was helpless to prevent it and just as I thought I was going to lose my feet, big Maurice Vemett and Bob Quick dashed on deck in their bare feet and underwear. Each man grabbed one of my shoulders and whisked me out of the water like I was a toy doll. I was shivering with cold. Maurice took over my watch and I stripped down and got into the warm bunk. Captain Mike LaFountain took a glass of hot water, dumped several different spices in it and forced me to drink it. That was a horrible tasting concoction, but I suffered no ill effects from the cold swim. I did miss my breakfast that morning.

The *Junior Murray* had many shortcomings, but we had a good crew and a happy ship.

Junior Murray, **fall of 1933.**
New London, N.Y. junction lock to change propellor.

Chapter 4

I worked for a short time on the *Dorothy* under Captain John Davidson of Fort Miller. The engineer was Peter Matte of Whitehall and the fireman was his son John, who were normally the engine room gang on the *Triton*. John was a barber and it was convenient to have a barber aboard ship. He ran the *Triton* barber shop for many years in Whitehall.

The *Dorothy* (built at Buffalo, N.Y. in 1899) had a steel hull and a wooden house that extended over the side decks to the rails on each side. As a result, there was a large stateroom aft and a large comfortable galley forward. The deckhand could walk up and down the side decks in a rain storm without getting wet.

This tug's draft was only about 6 ft. I was told that she was sent through the Chambly Canal in Canada with a tow. She was shallow enough to operate in that canal, but there must have been other drawbacks. She did not repeat the experiment and the barges continued to be towed by tractors.

Murray Transportation Company, or The Lake Champlain Despatch Company, whichever you prefer, was the only company doing general towing through the Champlain Canal since The Line had ceased operations. Some of the products carried on Murray scows and barges, as well as the few privately owned boats that still survived, were hay, lumber, clay, newsprint paper, iron ore, sand, brick and pulp wood. The Gulf Oil Co. oil barge *Osage* was towed from Gulfport on Staten Island to Burlington, Vt. on a regular basis. Other companies towed oil barges up to Lake Champlain ports. Standard Oil of New York operated a fleet of self-propelled tankers throughout the state. The smaller of these tankers, such as *Utica, Socony, Albany Socony* and *Buffalo Socony*, were used between Albany and ports on Lake Champlain. They had such men as Captain Bill Sweet of Plattsburgh, and Captain Coleman Smith of Fort Edward. These vessels operated at night as well as daytime on both the canal and the lake. Murray's tugs did the same, as had the tugs of The Line. No other tugboats operated at night in these waters with oil barges until about 1952.

It was said that Murray and The Cornell Steamboat Company had an unwritten agreement that Cornell would not do any towing in the Champlain Canal if Murray did not do any towing on the Hudson River. At the end of the 1933 season, the Murray fleet of tugs was tied up at the malt house at 120th Street, North Troy, waiting for Cornell to tow them to New York. The crews had been laid off and the engines laid up for the winter except for the *Defender*, whose engineers were just beginning to work on her. Cornell delayed so long that the fleet was frozen in. A small wooden tug was sent up to get them, but turned around at 112th street because of the ice. Cornell reported that a steel hull tug was not available just then and the fleet would have to remain icebound until Spring. That caused great anger in Murray's office and from that time on Murray did all of its own Hudson River towing. Cornell never entered the Champlain Canal.

The *Defender* was hurriedly put back together. A crew was rounded up and the steel hull was put to work breaking the ice. The fleet was taken in tow and headed for New York.

Bill Vandervoort of Waterford, engineer on the *Billy Murray*, was appointed to ride the fleet and I was appointed to help him. This was also a safety measure as it was dangerous for one man alone crawling from one tug to another. We were to keep the various tugs pumped out and to watch them in case they were cut through by the ice. *Dorothy* had a steel hull so we didn't worry about her, but kept a good watch on the wooden ships. The next morning *Dorothy* looked rather low in the water. On inspection we found many small water spouts in her coal bunkers. Apparently the ice had knocked rust spots off her hull and water was spraying into the hull. Luckily, her coal bunkers were empty. The water was pumped out and Bill and I began whittling pine plugs and driving them into the holes. We finally stopped all of the leaks, but it took a lot of plugs. Bill said there were as many plugs sticking up as there were quills on a porcupine.

We arrived in New York harbor on a cold dark evening. Bill and I were living in the galley on the *Billy Murray* and had everything closed up tight. The only place to see out was a small porthole on each side. I kept moving from one to the other looking out at the great number of vessels moving around us. The river seemed to be full of ferry boats dashing madly back and forth along with other unidentified red and green running lights heading in all directions. I marveled that so many vessels could operate without colliding. Those of you who are accustomed to the present quiet waters of the North River would find it difficult to visualize the heavy traffic that once was there.

The tow finally arrived at piers 5 and 6, East River and the office had a tug standing by. On our arrival this tug pulled a fleet of Murray's barges out of the slip and took them to another tie-up spot. Our tugboat fleet was put in their place and Murray's tugs were in a snug harbor for the winter.

That's the last I saw of *Dorothy*. She must have been sold or scrapped.

**The *Defender* assisting *Madeline Murray* with loaded iron ore tow.
The day after Thanksgiving, 1936.**

Chapter 5

The *Defender* (built at Baltimore, Md. in 1895) was the best looking of the old steamboats that I knew intimately. She must have been a beauty when on Lake Champlain for The Line, with a high pilot house, tall stack and masts, and a white hull. I knew her at a later time when she had been cut down for the canals.

The hull was steel with a wooden deck and a wooden house. A comfortable pilot house was on the upper deck whose windows were not the usual flat panes, but were curved to fit the shape of the house. When broken, they were very expensive to replace.

The interior of the pilot house, galley, engine room, and the quarters on deck, were lined with hardwood panels, beautifully varnished. I have seen its equal on no other tugboat. Many of these panels could be tilted out revealing a secret hiding place. I was told that during the Prohibition era many a bottle left Canada concealed in these spaces. I was also told that one trip the empty spaces beneath the pilot house windows were full of bottles so the windows could not be opened. Such smuggling was no longer done in my time. I do remember one barge loaded with Canadian Ale and topped off with a deck load of hay that came out of Canada. Two U.S. Border Patrolmen were put aboard to ride the boat to New York. The owner-captain of the barge received much advice about sinking the evidence off West Point, setting it on fire, etc. He did not try any of the suggestions. When the hay was removed in New York, the illegal booze was exposed. I do not remember what was done to the guilty man.

Living conditions aboard were good for a tug of this type. The pilot house was not used for sleeping so it made a good lounging area. Master and mate had the last room aft on the main deck. Between this and the engine room was a cabin for the engineers. The unlicensed men slept in the fo'csle (forecastle). This was roomy, equipped with lockers, and well ventilated. Under the pilot house was the dining area with a short hallway connecting it to the cooking area just behind it. This was far better than the cramped little galleys usually found on tugs of this size.

The engine was a fore and aft compound. It was so quiet you could sit in the engine room and converse in whispers. A fireman who had been transferred from one of the high pressure tugs to *Defender* was greatly impressed. His former tug had much vibration because of the single crank engine and was noisy because the spent steam was exhausted directly into the atmosphere. The change to the smooth-running engine was very noticeable. The fireman spread his arms out like wings and took a few steps down the deck in imitation of a soaring bird.

"The *Defender* not noisy," he said in accented English. "She go 'swoosh' and fly like a seagull."

He tried to give her this nickname but did not succeed.

Being a condensing engine, no steam was exhausted into the open air and there were no soot-filled drops of water from condensed steam raining down on one's head. The firemen who served the scotch boiler earned their 70 dollars per month for she was a hard steamer. The jet was usually blowing in the smoke stack to provide draft for the fires causing the discharge of small cinders from the stack. They were dry and would not polka-dot one's clothes as the exhaust rain did. Nevertheless, they were annoying and collected on deck if there was no wind to blow them away, another penalty for being what some New York harbor men called a "short stacker."

Her engine could be changed from ahead to reverse and back to ahead very quickly and with good power in each direction. I think that a pilot and an engineer, working in concert, could "back and fill" this tug with sufficient speed and power to slop water out of a filled pail sitting on deck.

Rudder power was not one of her strong points, but it was sufficient. The hand gear could bring a strong man to his knees if he tried to hold it hard over without using the becket. This problem was eliminated about 1935 when a good steam steering gear was installed. A single guard on her hull was a drawback for towing alongside but it helped make for speed running light. This was the fastest tug I every worked on. She could outrun the Staten Island Ferries if pushed.

Weatherbound in south wind. Gravelly Point, Lake Chanplain 1932.

During my 1932 school vacation I made my first trip on her as the galley helper (no pay). It was a pleasant cruise to St. Jean, P.Q. and return. The Champlain Canal locks were open only 16 hours per day that year so the tug had a single crew. We tied up every night and sometimes pitched horseshoes or tossed a baseball back and forth. We fished one evening on Lake Champlain and caught a mess of fish. The trip on Lake Champlain was particularly enjoyable. We dumped our water barrel and refilled it from the lake. The firemen had a small tin can to which they had affixed a wire bail and some strong cord. When they wanted a drink of cool water they just dipped it out of the lake.

In later years, I saw this tug after she had been converted to diesel power. I was shocked to discover that the beautiful hardwood panels had been covered with paint. The tug was later rebuilt and her looks changed completely. To me it looked like a monstrosity. What a terrible end for a beautiful ship.

The *Defender* was the best all around steamboat of her size that I ever knew.

George Godfrey, Marine Superintendent and "Nick" Desnoyers, pilot, 120th Street, North Troy. 1934

Chapter 6

120th Street, North Troy, New York 1934

The *Helen M. Murray* (built at Buffalo, N.Y. in 1882) was operated by the Line on Lake Champlain as the *Robert H. Cook* until she was purchased by the Murray company and taken to New York. The pilot house, smokestack, mast, davits, etc. which had been removed to get the ship under the canal bridges, were replaced. The ship was repainted, named the *Helen M. Murray*, and tied up. For the next six or more years, she remained as a threat to the Cornell Steamboat Co., which was then doing all of Murray's towing of deckscows and barges on the Hudson River. In the Spring of 1934, after Cornell had allowed Murray's tugs to be frozen in the fall before, she was brought out of mothballs and placed into service.

My uncle, Clayton Godfrey, was hired as Master and George Smith of Kingston as Mate. I wanted river and harbor experience, so I asked for a deckhand's job and was hired. What a change! I now had more coal to shovel, more ashes to haul, more area to keep clean, heavier lines to handle, for the same 70 dollars per month with no pay for overtime.

At first we towed oil barges between New York and Troy where the canal tugs took over. It immediately became apparent that this tug did not carry enough fresh water for the boiler to enable her to pull heavy tows into or out of New York Harbor. The engine was not equipped to reuse the water condensed from the steam of the exhaust. Having always operated in fresh water before, that had never mattered, but now it was very important.

The pilots and deckhands were transferred to *Defender,* and *Helen M. Murray* was put in the shipyard at Kingston, N.Y. The large forecastle space was converted to a huge fresh water tank and another tank was added to the stern space. One can get an idea of the size and capacity of these tanks by looking at photos and comparing the freeboard when full of water to others when the tanks are not full. The tug was put back into service with George Smith as her Master, a position he held for the rest of her career.

She replaced *Defender* as the principal Hudson River tug and began work on the tows but there was still a problem. With very heavy tows, such as with many iron ore scows, she could

D. L. & W. R. R. tug *Bath*

barely make it into New York without running out of coal or water. We took on both of these necessities at Burns Brothers, Pier 5, Hoboken. Several times we were unable to deliver the tow to its destination but had to hang up the tow and run for fuel and water. The water tanks would be nearly empty and the fireman sweeping the last of the coal from the bunkers. The engineer would have to decide which one was more important to take aboard first.

When coaling up at Pier 5, Hoboken, I would see all of the D.L. & W. Railroad tugs which were dispatched from this area. My father had often told stories of these tugs for he had worked as a deckhand in a roustabout crew on these vessels in 1918. His all-time favorite tugboat, rated above all others, was the *Bath*.

Taking in coal and water at Burns Brothers, Pier 5, Hoboken, N.J.

The boiler on *Helen Murray* consumed a great amount of fuel. It was not particularly hard to keep up steam, but the great heat in the fireroom and the amount of coal used each six hours would kill off the firemen. Bill McCourt, the boss in the New York office, used to ask,

"How can two men shovel that much coal in two days?"

Later, another fireman was added. One man who seemed to have very little trouble making steam was a skinny kid from

Brooklyn named Marshall. He was very good, but he was on in the fall months when it was cooler. I don't remember his last name but he later became an engineer for McAllister and his brother was a tugboat pilot.

There was no crowding aboard this ship. Galley and dining room forward, were spacious, sleeping quarters were very good. The Master and Mate had the room in the rear of the pilot house. On the main deck aft was a large room the full width of the deckhouse for the cook and firemen. In one corner was a small room with a toilet. Opening off of the large room was a room for the engineers on the starboard side, and a room for the deckhands on the port side. One old timer told me that when this tug was on Lake Champlain, Captain Sweeney was Master and his wife was cook. The captain had the room in the pilot house and his wife had the three rooms aft, including the toilet. All of the rest of the crew were in the fo'csle. He also told me that the cook would permit no one in to eat unless he had a shirt on over his undershirt. The firemen were not permitted to enter the dining room wearing their dirty work shoes but had to wear slippers. Sounds very unfair, if true.

The *Robert H. Cook*, like other old steam boats, did not have an electric generator when built. The owners, The Line, having obtained a D.C. generator and a steam towing engine, asked Capt. Sweeney which one he wanted for his ship, the *Cook*. Naturally, he chose the generator so he could have electric lights and, more importantly, a searchlight. The deckhands could still haul the hawser by hand. The towing engine was installed on *Defender*. When Murray bought her the engine was removed.

I took pride in the condition of the *Helen M. Murray* and worked hard to keep her looking good. The toughest part of the job was the hawsers which had to be pulled by hand up over the high fantail, one deckhand to each hawser. This was exhausting. By the time the hawsers were again made fast to the stern bitts after shortening up, the deckhands would be gasping for breath. When Nick Desnoyers was Mate he used to stand on the upper deck aft and needle us. He would say,

"Whistle me a little tune now boys."

We couldn't whistle if our lives depended on it. My opposite deckhand was a lean lanky man about 60 years old called Minoon LaFontain, who managed to get his hawser in despite his age. Minoon hailed from Champlain, N.Y., and was a good shipmate. He was a former canal boat owner and barge captain. His two sons, Clarence and Ozzie, were tugboat captains.

The night watches in the pilot house with Smitty were enjoyable for he would tell tales about the Cornell Steamboat Co., the Day Line, and the night boats. George taught me more about the Hudson River than any other pilot.

The North River in 1934 was a busy place full of all types of vessels; excursion steamers, ocean going freighters, passenger ships, ferry boats, and a great many other harbor craft. Eight or more ferry routes operated between New Jersey and Manhattan with several boats on each run, mostly owned by the different railroads in the area. A colored-light on a mast amidships distinguished which line a ferry belonged to. As I remember it, four railroads were carrying lights of red, white, green, or blue.

Fleets of tugs, carfloats, lighters, covered scows, etc., were operated in the North River by Central RR of New Jersey, Erie RR, Pennsylvania RR, D.L. & W. RR, and New York Central RR. Penn RR built special tugs for shifting work at their piers. These strange craft were pointed at each end like a tug with two

Double-ended Pennsylvania R.R. shifting tug

bows and no stern and operated like a ferry boat for the man in the wheelhouse didn't need to turn his vessel around. He merely turned himself around and steered in the opposite direction.

The first time Smitty asked me to steer when heading up the North River, I was reluctant to take the wheel. His instructions made sense to me.

"Ignore all traffic except ships and other hawser tows. They will all see that you have a tow and will go around you."

This proved to be good advice. No one at the time would have imagined that the North River would become the deserted waterway it is today.

There have been many changes in the harbor and also in the city. When I was deckhand on the *Helen M. Murray*, and working in New York, I would go shore for an evening and the other deckhand would take my watch. Early morning generally found me waiting in the dark, on the end of some pier, for the tug to arrive. Often I would sleep there while waiting. The waterfront was a tough neighborhood, but I was never molested. On a cold or rainy night, when I had time to kill, I would go to the nearest subway station, deposit my nickel, and stretch out on the wooden bench. The worst that ever happened to me there was having the soles of my shoes smartly rapped by a police officer. When that happened I boarded a train and took a ride until sufficient time had elapsed, and then returned to the pier. Today such actions would be very foolhardy.

I had one experience on this ship that I never forgot. We were southbound, about 3 a.m., with the oil barge *Osage* in ballast on our port side. The Mate, whose name does not appear in this book, attempted to pass on the west side of a downbound tow. The tug struck bottom on the starboard side and this caused her to roll over to port. I had been asleep in my room, and, having been rolled out of my bunk, I dove out of the window and landed on my stomach on the edge of the oil barge. The coaming of the deck house came down on my back. I quickly wriggled out from under, losing some skin from my back. The coaming then came down onto the deck of the barge. If I had been one second slower,

Gulf barge *Osage* on port side of tug.
Other barge thought to be *Rockland #1*. 1934

I would have been crushed. It is almost unbelievable that this high tug could list over far enough to lay her deckhouse on the deck that was only five or six feet above the water. Standing on the deck of the barge, shocked and stunned, I could only wonder how that tall black smokestack could be so far from perpendicular and still not break off. There had been many parts of the headline, backing line, and stern line put out. None of these had parted and this prevented the tug from capsizing. The barge, maintaining headway, pulled the tug around and off the bottom. She became erect again but was barely afloat.

Conditions aboard were not good. The galley was a mess, pots and pans scattered around, and many dishes broken. The bilges were overflowing with seawater and the crankpits as well. Coal had come out of the bunkers and covered the floor plates in the fireroom to the level of the fire doors. We drifted in the river while getting things straightened out. The water had to be pumped out. The fireman had to dig coal out of the ash pits so air could get to the fires for draft. He also had to dig enough coal away from the front of the boiler so he had a place to stand while working. It was fortunate that the lower doors of the engine room and fire room had been closed and only one bunker plate off. She would not have survived any more water coming aboard.

No one was injured, but had she rolled farther there would have been. The cook and firemen were trapped in their room because an unfastened bedspring and mattress had slid into and jammed the doorway. In the dark, with the great tilt of the deck, they could not get themselves oriented to get the doorway cleared. The assistant engineer, Ben Balzer of Waterford, could not get out of the engine room. The metal deck was inclined so sharply that he could not climb it to the high side. He called to the fireman, Al Fontaine, to get the chief out of the cabin. Ben shouted just in time. Al was standing on the high side of the hull and was just about to jump overboard. The ship returned to an even keel and the Chief was able to get out of his room. The Chief at the time was George Goyette, who lived in Canada. When the tug listed over, the wooden deck house was wracked so that the door of the engineer's room could not be opened. The Chief was about 65 years old and could not get through the windows on the high side of his cabin. He sure did shout for help. When he was able to open his door, he came into the engine room, very scared, and very angry. The Mate came down to the engine room and sat down on the locker. Then the action started. The Chief was a short paunchy man, clad only in long-handled drawers, baggy at the knees, and otherwise mis-shapened. His scant gray hair was tousled and his face livid with rage. The steel deck was too hot for his bare feet, so he kept hopping from one foot to the other like someone doing a pagan dance. All this time he was shaking his fists at the Mate and shouting insults and imprecations in a mixture of Canadian-French and broken English. It seems very comical in retrospect but was not so at the time, especially for the Mate.

The Chief's fear is understandable to me. My own fear lasted for more than a year. Anytime my ship listed over I was out of bed and running to get clear of the house. This caused me to wonder if sometime I might jump overboard before I was fully awake. My deckhand partners didn't mind. I always got up and helped coal up and didn't return to my bunk until the ship was on an even keel again. It is interesting to note the difference in men.

Our Captain, George Smith, was rolled out of bed. When the ship returned to level, he came out on the upper deck, looked around, and went beck to bed, deciding that morning would be time enough to get details.

There was another story about an engineer on the *Helen Murray* that made the rounds at a later time. Ben Balzer was Chief and Ed DeLorme of Hudson Falls was Assistant Engineer. Ed had injured his hand as a fireman and the last two fingers of one hand were removed and also half of his palm. The tug had tied up at 120th Street in Troy and was going to remain overnight. Ed was going to go home for the night and his brother-in-law had come down with a car to bring him home. In the meantime, that afternoon, a fireman had gone up to the bar at 120th Street and Second Avenue. He was drinking and exchanged some hard nasty words with some of the bar's patrons before returning to the tug. Three angry people decided to teach him a lesson. When it got dark they went down to the river bank and hid in the shadows of the bushes hoping to ambush the fireman. There was a light barge canal boat tied up to the shore. Ed DeLorme and his brother-in-law jumped down off this barge and were immediately jumped by the three characters who were after the fireman. There was quite a melee at the foot of the street. The brother-in-law was knocked cold and the three assailants broke off and ran up the street. Ed brought his friend back to consciousness and, having seen the three re-enter the bar, decided the brawl was not over. The two went up the street, into the saloon, and challenged the three attackers. Ed reached out, grabbed the leader by his shirt front, pulled him forward and then drove him back with a good hard fist to the mouth, displacing some teeth. The other two immediately departed in haste and the war was over. The leader was supposedly one of the toughest characters from South Troy with two of his cronies.

The story was circulated throughout the area that the bully of South Troy could not handle a one-handed tugboat man. It was printed in *The Green Sheet*, a scandal sheet published in Troy at the time. This small paper once carried an ad by the notorious Mame Fay and her bordello, near the Troy railroad station,

offering special attention to college students and traveling sales-
men. The death of this well-known madam was noted in Walter
Winchell's column with the comment that many big time politi-
cians attended the funeral.

One pair of Engineers (Ben Balzer and Charley Shinvier)
used to tease me a great deal. As was usual, the youngest crew
member got the most
hazing. I knew it was
all in fun but occasion-
ally they would get me
worked up, and I
would declare that
when I got my Masters
license I would go to
work on their tug and
my first official act
would be to fire them
both. Of course they
were delighted to get
me raving like that. In
calmer moments I used
to tell them that when I
became wealthy I was
going to build a tug-
boat. On this ship the
deckhands would have
the best quarters and
the engineers the poor-
est. All pay would be
equal. The boilers
would be fired by oil so

there would be no coal to shovel nor ashes to haul. There would
be no white paint to be scrubbed and all brass would be painted
over. My ideal tugboat would be christened *Deckhands' Paradise*.

Helen M. Murray was not such a heaven for deckhands,
but I spent a very enjoyable season aboard her.

Chapter 7

Watuppa was an all steel tugboat (built at Port Richmond, N.Y. in 1906) used for towing coal barges coastwise.

I went down to Pier 5 East River early one morning hoping to land a deckhand's job. *Watuppa* pulled in and I was hired. There were no ashes to haul on this ship as she was equipped with an ash siphon. The fireman shoveled the ashes into a hopper down below and then pumped them overboard. A steam capstan was used to pull in the heavy hawsers. This was still hard work as the manila rope was very large and watersoaked. When towing two barges or two

Watuppa in Rondout Creek

mud scows there would be an intermediate hawser to handle as well.

Watuppa was available for any type of towing that was needed. While I was in her crew she did just about every kind of tugboat job except towing railroad carfloats. She worked on the Hudson River and Long Island Sound and did general harbor towing. Once in a while she would dock or undock a ship and occasionally tow mud to sea. For a time she towed oil barges between Philadelphia and New York. This was no treat for me because I had a weak stomach in rough weather.

The engineers, like others of their kind, were concerned about the supply of fresh water for the boiler. The water had to be used sparingly when towing on the coast. I still remember the tiny Chief Engineer shaking a wrench under the nose of a big fireman and warning him not to open the jet in the smokestack unless he wanted his head bashed in.

It was a very cold winter and Long Island Sound froze over. Because of the steel hull, *Watuppa* was given many jobs in the ice. One trip was made down the Sound and back with a small self-propelled Gulf Oil barge. The little tanker was built of steel but did not have enough power to go through the ice. The tug put a hawser on the tanker's stem and towed her through the ice. The Hackensack River was also frozen and we were once stuck there for several days. The hull was not the proper shape to make a good icebreaker. She would wedge in the ice instead of breaking it. This caused her ribs on each side to be pushed in. All of her ribs on each side had to be replaced from the forward quarter bitts to the fire room doors.

Sleeping quarters for the officers were okay but the unlicensed men were all in the fo'csle. Sleep was very difficult down there when running through the ice. The steel hull really boomed when hit by the ice chunks.

Watuppa was far from the ideal harbor tug. She was a wet ship when towing coastwise. Hudson River and Long Island Sound towing suited her much better.

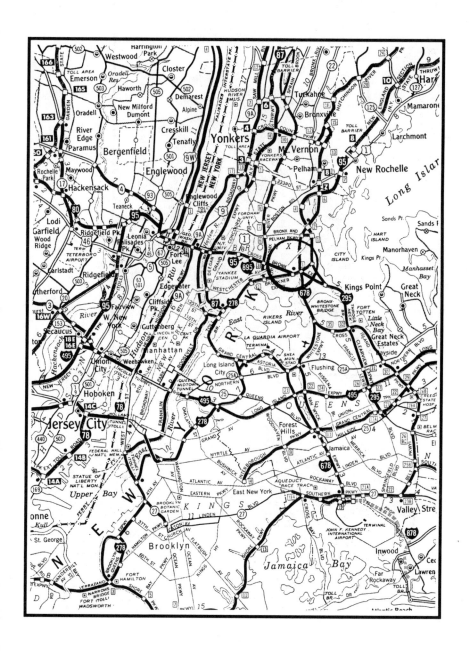

Watuppa having hull repaired in Staten Island. 1936

Stuck in ice.
Hackensack River, February 1936

Chapter 8

120th Street, North Troy 1936

About 1936 the harbor tug *Madeline Meseck* (built at Tottenville, N.Y. in 1916) was purchased and renamed *Madeline Murray*. She had a wooden hull built by Brown of Staten Island, a Heipenhauser boiler, and Sullivan engine, a combination very popular in her time. The smokestack and mast were shortened, the pilot house lowered, and she was ready for the canal. A double crew was put aboard headed by Clayton Godfrey, Master, and Bob Quick, Chief Engineer.

After a couple of days of doing a few short jobs in the harbor she was given a tow bound up the Hudson. This tow consisted of light barge canal boats and bound for Canada to load newsprint paper. The tug would leave them in St. Jean, P.Q., where they would be taken through the Chambly Canal by tractors. Also in the tow were two eel boats, flimsy craft, not much to look at and almost flush with the water. They were really floating fish tanks that the water flowed through freely. These eel boats would be left in St. Jean. Eels would be caught throughout the summer, put in the floating tank, and in the autumn, when full, they would be towed to New York. Live eels were sold from these boats during the winter and in the spring they would again be towed to Canada. This might have been the last year of the eel boats.

The trip up the Hudson and through the Champlain Canal was uneventful. The captain decided that because of the weather on the broad lake, it was not safe to take the tow across, so the boats were taken into Snake Den and tied up to the shore with a line around a tree. This place received a lot of use by northbound tows in bad weather. Snake Den was an indentation in the west shore just past Calico Rock and before Diamond Island. The mountains slope right down to the water's edge so the whole bay is very deep. When tied up in there, one has no idea of the direction or velocity of the wind. Walking ashore was discouraged by the steep land and the tales of rattlesnakes. We never had much success fishing there and the only outdoor recreation was swimming in water that was very cold. Poker was a popular pastime.

The weather improved and the tug and tow left Snake Den and crossed the broad lake to Rouses Point. We passed the Rouses Point bridge, then under construction, and went down the Richelieu River. Early in the season the lake level is high and consequently the river was higher and the current stronger than in midsummer. There was a small narrow bridge at LaColle. It was a swingbridge and the operator lived nearby. To swing the bridge open, he pushed a turnstile in circles, making many turns before the bridge was fully open. Often his little children would help him in this work. As it was the first trip of the year the tow was dropped through this bridge. The tug took in the hawsers and put one hawser out on the stern of the last barge. Then, working against the current, the tug and tow were maneuvered so as to allow them to drift slowly and safely backward through the bridge. The hawsers were then returned to the head boat and the trip resumed.

On arrival at St. Jean the same procedure was used at the bridge there. The mate and his deckhand went in a rowboat and ran lines ashore from the barges as they went through the bridge. The bargemen then snubbed with these lines and brought the tow into the terminal wall out of the river current. Later, when the river level was lower, the tug and tow went head on through these bridges.

There were no places to coal up on this northern run so the company had car loads of coal dumped on the railroad pier at Rouses Point. A wheelbarrow was left there and some planks. In the Spring, when the lake was high, it took some effort to push a full wheelbarrow up that plank to the tug's rail. Everyone except the captain, chief, and cook were expected to take part in this exercise although some exceptions were made. It was hard work swinging those big coal scoops. The company sweetened the pot by paying each of us $.50 an hour. Truckloads of coal were also dumped on the canal terminal at Whitehall for our use. The same $.50 per hour was paid but we always found enough unemployed locals to shovel the coal. This was just about the last year that Mr. William Cody was employed by the State of New York as Harbormaster for Whitehall. He was a fine gentlemen, well liked by the boatmen, and always ready to help any of us who needed it.

Having made a couple of trips into Canada, the *Madeline* was put on the iron ore run between Port Henry and Troy, N.Y. The *Helen Murray* brought light scows from New York to Troy. The canal tugs would each make up a tow of four scows, which was a double locking, and head north. They were large scows with high cabins. The first low bridge encountered was the railroad bridge which crossed the canal and the river to the paper mill above Lock #5. (This bridge was removed for scrap metal during World War II). The scows were tied up to the trees along the canal bank and canal water pumped into each in turn for ballast. The ballasting was accomplished by using a steam siphon, which was a length of large, heavy iron pipe sufficient to reach from the deck of a scow into the canal water. It was powered by steam pressure from the tug blowing through a head on the top of the pipe. This worked well but was heavy to move from scow to scow. When all the boats were ballasted and able to go under the bridge the tow would proceed on.

On arrival at Port Henry, the water would have to be

siphoned back out of the scows. A few of them, equipped with gasoline pumps, would pump themselves out. Later on an old barge was fitted with large pumps and tied up to the iron ore dock at Port Henry to be used to pump water ballast out of the scows.

Sometimes a tug would have two of these fleets (8 scows) to tow up or down the lake. Four scows was the limit in the canal because the state allowed only two lockings for each tug. They were one thousand ton scows fully loaded to ten feet. Some of them would have the deck awash amidship when in fresh water. They would have a few inches of freeboard when in the more buoyant salt water.

The pilots on these small low-powered steamboats deserve credit for their work with these heavy tows. No other group of men had the local knowledge to handle this work as well as they did. The river locks had short approach walls as well as other problems. Locks #3 and #2 were the most difficult. Below Lock #3 the water from the paper mill rushed across the river and through the piers on the other side. It was impossible to keep the tows off of the heavy wooden boom along these piers. The pilots would put the tow on the boom as soon as possible so as to avoid doing damage by hitting it with force. As soon as the scow was on the boom the tug tried to pull the tow away from it. This was impossible until the head scow was through the cross current. In the meantime, the tug had to be pulling away from the piers so as not to get pushed into them by the current. The sterns of the little steamboats were pretty close to the piers and it would look as though the propeller or rudder would hit, but it never happened. The tow had to be pulled off the boom before reaching the lower end where there was hard rock. The first boat would then take a dive for the concrete pier on the west side of the river and would be pulled back into line and headed through the abutments of the old Mechanicville bridge.

Meanwhile, the tug *Comstock* would be on the tail end of the tow helping to keep things in shape and to straighten the tow for the bridge. This little steamboat was owned by the Vandervoort family of Waterford. She was the handiest tug I ever saw but was very small. New York State hired this little tug to help tows in and out of Lock #3. She didn't work very hard so she was kept in immaculate condition. Her crew was Louis Vandervoort, Captain; his brother Al Vandervoort, Engineer; and Willie Gandreau, Deckhand.

Entering Lock #2 there was also some current to contend with. The short approach wall on the west side had some piers extending out from it, also with a wooden boom. The water at the end of the wall ran through these piers because of the powerhouse drawing water. Again the tow had to be put on the boom as soon as possible to avoid hitting it too hard. When the tow got onto the wall the head boat generally tried to hit the bullnose. The rest of the trip down was routine.

Another place where one had to be careful with loaded tows was Northumberland. The tugs came down through the bridge at dead slow speed. This made it easier to turn the tow to the right around the first bend. When this turn was complete the tail end of the tow would be swinging downriver with the current behind it. This made it very difficult to turn the tow to the left, behind the piers and into the landcut. The little steamboat would be skimming along the piers, running wide open to break the head scow back to port.

Again, these men deserve credit for their good work on those heavy tows with those low-powered tugs. Some years later Moran underbid Murray for the iron ore towing. The *Kevin Moran* and the *F.Y. Robertson* were put on the job. Later the towing was done with tugs chartered from John E. Matton. One of the locktenders kept track of the tonnage carried. He wondered how Moran could make any money on this job when he underbid the contract but brought out less ore. The Moran scows carried 750 tons. Although the scows were smaller, each tow was split up at Lock #4. The tugs would take only two scows at a time down river and then return for the other two. Murray's men had always taken four, Moran also hired a fleet captain for each four scows to get off and take lines at each lock. The big advantage held by the new tugs on the job was the scows. Not only were they smaller, they had low cabins and did not have to be ballasted. This was a great saving in time.

The *Madeline Murray* normally left her loaded tow in Troy and started back with a light one. A couple of times she was sent down river with eight ore scows to change tows with the river tug. It was immediately apparent that she did not have the power for this work.

I got my pilot's license in July, a second class license because I was not 21 years old. I could be pilot in charge of a watch, but could not be master of a ship up to 150 gross tons as could a first class pilot. On my 21st birthday, a first class license was automatically in effect. Business was good, men were being hired, and I was promoted to mate on *Madeline Murray*. The first few trips down through Locks #3 and #2 caused me to worry a little, but thanks to the training I had received things turned out well.

One event worth telling happened while on the iron ore run. The *Madeline Murray*, with a tow of light scows strung out behind her, was bound for Port Henry. We had just gone through the Crown Point Bridge about eleven p.m. when the wind began to pick up. It rapidly increased in strength, blowing straight down the lake. Clayt headed for the canal terminal at Port Henry. He hoped to get in the lee of the pier with a line on the dock. The tow could then hang behind us in safety.

The wind kept increasing and we were making no headway. Bob Quick broke the seal on the safety valve and put some more steam pressure on the boiler. The engine was working hard with plenty of steam, but the wind was too strong. Finally Clayt had the deckhand stock the anchor and throw it overboard fastened to a headline. All of our efforts were in vain. The wind blew tug and tow stern first up into Bulwagga Bay until the last boat fetched up on the shore. We could then hold our own. I spent my morning watch with the engine running, steering into the wind but going nowhere. The wind gradually abated and we were able to move when daylight came. A narrow gap had been made through the old piling at the mouth of the bay to let Socony tankers get to their dock. The amazing thing about our adventure was that the complete tug and tow were blown stern first through this gap without touching anything.

We had no means to pick up the anchor so a wood fender was tied to the line to mark its location. We steamed over to the ore dock with the tow. The wind was estimated to have been between 90 and 100 mph. The barge with the pumps had been wrecked. The wind had broken her loose from the dock and wrecked her on the lake shore. The boss decided it was unsafe to go back for the anchor, so it was abandoned. For all I know, it is still there.

The *Madeline Murray* was a decent handling ship with a steam steering gear and good rudder power. These were advantages when she pushed an oil barge. The pilot had to watch her closely when running light as she was extremely wild. Her quarters were not great but were all on deck.

The best thing about this tug was her captain and her chief engineer, Clayton Godfrey and Bob Quick. These two men were buddies and both extremely capable in their jobs. They insisted that others do their work well also. Both were practical jokers and always had something going on. One time Bob put a little limburger cheese on the steering wheel. There was just enough to make the pilots' hands smell a little. Clayt never mentioned it but shortly thereafter goodly amount of this odoriferous cheese was smeared on the hot main engine. That really made a smell! As some people would say, "Bad enough to gag a maggot."

These two men often went ashore together and patronized the bars. Bob's oft stated ambition was to get that big red-head loaded and then call the boss saying your engineer is ready but your captain is drunk." Bob never succeeded. His drinking partner had nearly unlimited capacity.

I was mate but the youngest man aboard ship and the two hecklers called me "the young whippersnapper." My life was very interesting because of the tricks they played on me. We had a competent, congenial crew, and two good men for leaders. That made for a happy ship.

Barge is being towed along western part of the Erie Canal. Boys or men lead the mules which pull the boats.

Chapter 9

The *Billy Murray* (built at Camden, N.J. in 1908) like many steam tugs of her time, had no great talent and some drawbacks. She had a good wooden hull, her second boiler, and an engine of only moderate power. There was no water tank in her stern so the fantail was rather high out of water, part of the reason for her poor rudder power. The hand gear was not as heavy as some, but it was a long way from power steering.

In 1937, I went aboard this tug as mate. Bill Whalen, of Whitehall and Waterford was Master, and Bill Vandervoort, of Waterford, was Chief Engineer. The Assistant Engineer on my watch was Ed DeLorme of Hudson Falls and my deckhand was Matt Taft of Whitehall.

We were working between Troy, N.Y. and St. Jean, P.Q. and the summertime towing on Lake Champlain was pleasant work. The weather was usually good without the winds which appeared in the fall. Midsummer heat was not a problem on the lake as it sometimes was in the canal. The cool bunkrooms and the quiet hawser tow made for good sleeping. We sometimes had a night in Whitehall because the pilots would not leave after dark when northbound, the excuse being that we could not run the marshes after dark. The boss in New York thought it very strange that the darkness did not bother us when we were southbound. The excuse now was that when northbound it was more dangerous because we had the current behind us. We all knew, and I'm sure the boss did also, that the force of the current was negligible. In fact, the marshes were easier to navigate than the narrow lake. Nothing could be done by the big wheels in the company to change the situation. There were only six licensed pilots with the knowledge necessary to run the Richelieu River. They all worked for Murray and all stood by their guns on this issue. I was the last addition to this elite group and I was the only mate in the company with a pilot's license for Lake Champlain which guaranteed me a job. When there was a lull in business some tugs would be temporarily laid up. I would be knocked down to deckhand, but I would still receive Mate's pay. This was to keep me from going somewhere else to work. My ego was inflated by this treatment as I was very young. I now realize how much more knowledge and experience was needed before I would be truly worthy of such treatment.

The tug never left St. Jean with a tow at night. The Richelieu was supposed to have a channel of 6'6" minimum depth. Actually, in midsummer it was about 8' if you knew where to go. Eight feet two inches was about the lightest draft that the *Billy Murray* could be trimmed to. This meant that in the shallowest part of the river (a section we called "The Stumps"), we ran dead slow because the propeller would hit. Many blades from the old cast iron propellers were left in the river. The channel was marked by wooden spar buoys painted red or black, but in the spring these buoys would show no color because the ice had scraped it all off. It didn't matter to us as we steered by landmarks and ignored the buoys, sometimes going behind them. Bill Whalen gave me many tips about pilotage on this river.

The layovers in St. Jean were enjoyed very much. Several

times we played baseball alongside the terminal wall joined by young Canadian men and boys and we had a fine time. Many of these people could not speak English and I knew no French, which made for an interesting ball game. Ed DeLorme, our engineer, was fluent in both languages and acted as interpreter.

Once when the *Defender* was tied up there, the cook decided to go up to the dairy store for some fresh milk and butter. A crew member told him that the clerk would not understand English so the cook must repeat a phrase in French that this crew member gave him. These words were not the kind you would say to your Sunday school teacher. The cook went to the dairy store and, as luck would have it, was waited on by a woman. The offending crew member had not expected this development. The cook repeated the phrase that he rehearsed. The woman paused for a second, then said,

"I speak English. Please tell me what you want. Tell your friend who taught you those words he should be ashamed."

She was a nice lady. I found the people of our neighboring country to be very courteous and friendly.

Life aboard these small ships was confining and monotonous. Standing watches of six hours on and six hours off, day and night, day after day, week after week, with no time off, could drive a man crazy. Particularly hard hit were the married men who greatly missed their wives and children. I would occasionally work a twenty-four hour shift in the canal and let the captain go home for awhile. At the next opportunity he would do the same for me. This was illegal as pilots were forbidden by law to work more than thirteen hours in any twenty-four hour period. The engineers and deckhands did the same thing. The cook might be allowed some time off by the deckhands. Because of the hard work involved, the firemen were unable to this. If we sometimes became over exuberant when given a night ashore it should be understood and excused.

Nights on Lake Champlain were often very black. We had no luxury, such as radar, and our compasses were never compensated by a professional adjuster. By noting the compass heading and times in daylight, we had an idea of what courses to steer on a dark night or in fog. Good night vision is a great asset to a pilot. I soon learned to close one eye when lighting a cigarette at night. Thus I only destroyed for a time the night vision capability of one eye instead of both.

Billy Murray, assisted by *Junior Murray* with 23 boat tow
southbound on Lake Champlain. 1937

With a tow on long hawsers the tug was very steady. This allowed me an extra half hour of sleep when on the broad lake. At five a.m., I would put the becket on the steering wheel, sit on the stool, lay my head on the wheel, and go to sleep. The cook would ring the breakfast bell at 5:30, awakening me and I would then make the small adjustment necessary to put the tug back on course. At the slow speed we traveled we could never get far enough off course to be in any danger.

The work changed that fall when the *Billy Murray* was given an oil barge to push. The barge was tied up at Waterford terminal. I went over to it with the tug in the afternoon to cable the tug up behind it. Having been away from this type of work for awhile, the barge looked as if it were a city block long. I wrestled the tug and barge up through "The Flight." The hand gear was not ideal for this job and I found that the rudder power was not all that it should be. Lack of sufficient rudder power was a constant problem at such places as Medina Bend on the sixty mile level, and Shithouse Bend east of Baldwinsville. Medina Bend was expected to give us trouble so we were very careful there. The other one surprised me. The first time we came to this bend, bound east with the barge in ballast, we did not do very well. The tug and barge wound up sliding along the shore on the outside of the bend and being battered by the trees overhanging the river. Later trips were made with more care and better success. I didn't know who gave this river bend its name, or why, but it was appropriate.

Nighttime operation was difficult because we did not have the proper searchlights. It was better in the Mohawk River because we could run without lights. The buoys then were lit by kerosene lanterns and showed up well when properly maintained. The buoy tenders did not keep them as well in the cold fall as they did in the summer. At night it was necessary to know where the bow corners of the barge were when no searchlight was lit. A narrow strip would be cut from a tin can and fastened to each of the running lights on the bow of the barge. Theses would project out far enough so as to reflect a little of the light back to the pilot. The bow corners of the barge could then be discerned without using a searchlight. This was a necessity when meeting other vessels who would be blinded if we used a searchlight. Some men would also put a small stick, painted white, in front of the white light. This was visible at night and showed where the center of the barge was. It helped when going through a guard gate and also when heading for a distant light at night.

We had only one searchlight and it was not much good, mounted on the bow of the barge with control lines back to the pilot house. It did not throw light very far ahead. When tugs first started pushing barges at night in the canal, they all used this system of one searchlight. Only one bank of the canal landcut could be lighted at one time so the light needed to be swung back and forth frequently. Also with the searchlight on the bow, there was no way to light up the length of the barge on each side. It soon became customary to carry two good searchlights on the barge. They were mounted on on each side halfway back or on the stern quarter, which proved more efficient. Our tug had not been pushing oil barges so was not properly equipped. Nevertheless, we did the work and did no damage. The captain and I were both glad to see the season end on that job.

Reference to the *Billy Murray* does not give me a feeling of nostalgia. She was just another old steamboat that plugged away at whatever job was given her until she wore out and was superseded by modern workboats. The Murray tugboats soon came upon hard times. The Canadians built self-propelled vessels to carry the newsprint paper to New York which had been the most lucrative of Murray's work. Iron ore from Port Henry was no longer shipped by water. There was no other shipping on Lake Champlain except oil. The old steamboats could not compete with the more modern diesels and Murray's tugs faded from the picture.

**Author's father George F. Godfrey as Master of the
Lake Champlain steamboat *Ticonderoga*.**

Chapter 10

The *Newark*

In the spring of 1938, I heard the Callahan Construction Company of Texas had the contract to deepen the Mohawk River from Lock #10, Cranesville, to Lock #8, Schenectady. This company chartered the equipment from American Pipe and Construction Co. of Kingston, N.Y., to do the work which required a hydraulic dredge, two dipper dredges, tug *Newark*, motor launch *Florence*, assorted dump scows, and other gear.

I applied for a steering job on the *Newark* but was told that they had enough men for two shifts, but if they decided to add a third crew, I could have the job. In the meantime, a job as deckhand was available on *Dipper Dredge #4* which I accepted.

The work began in Cranesville 32 miles from my home in Troy, so transportation was needed. I bought my first car, a 1929 Essex Super Six Coupe, for twenty-five dollars. A fireman from Watervliet and an engineer from Cohoes was working on the same job. My car always left before theirs in case of a breakdown. As it happened, my jalopy had no problems but the others did, so I took them to work when they had car trouble. At the end of the year, I traded my car for twenty-five dollars.

The dredge work suited me fine. The eight hour day/forty hour week seemed like a vacation after the long hours I had been working. A workman of that day who received one dollar per hour was considered to be very well paid. My rate was $1.04 per hour, payable in cash, once a week. Who could ask for anything more?

The dredge deckhand provided, along with many other duties, a ferry service between the dredge and the shore using a square ended workboat. I can't call it a rowboat because it had no rowlocks. It was propelled by a single oar over the stern. This was called sculling and was the first new skill I had to master. I have heard of a flakey person "...rowing a boat with only one oar in the water." We did it routinely.

After two or three days my job was changed to scowman which required me to ride the scows to the spoil area, dump the pockets, and then rewind them on the way back to the dredge. The scowman had more contact with the tugboat, which I liked. The reason for the change of jobs was that if I were placed on the tug it would have a less disruptive effect on the dredge crew. As it happened, I only relieved the tug captains a few days all summer.

A short time later, the boss decided that the third crew was not needed on the tug so there would be no steering job for me. I was now given the job of oiler on *Dredge #4,* possibly to keep me happy and available if needed on the tug. If so, the move was successful. My duties were to care for the swinging engine, hoisting engine, spud engines, and assist the deckhand when needed. The craneman took care of the crowding engine and the fireman took care of the stern spud engine. My past curiosity about the engines on the old steamboats was now of benefit to me. Caring for the steam engines, under the supervision of the dredge operator, was no great chore. My job was the easiest one on the dredge and I was happy in my work.

Callahan Construction Co. was paying us Great Lakes scale of union wages. In order to avoid labor problems, the workers were compelled to join the appropriate union. As an oiler,

I had to join the dredge workers union. As tugboat captain, I had to join the Licensed Tugmen's Protective Association. I was already a member of Local 333 UMD of ILA, a tugboat union. Paying dues in three unions was the only bad part of the job.

Dipper Dredge # 4

That fall, the job was shut down for the winter and most of the men laid off. The *Newark* was cut down to one crew and given the job of towing all floating equipment to Rondout Creek to lay up for the winter. A few days later the superintendent on the job called at my house to tell me the regular captain had a disagreement with the company and quit. He wanted me to finish up the job. I agreed, went aboard the *Newark*, and began bringing the equipment to Troy Terminal. The tow was being made up there to go to Rondout.

The *Newark*, being a dredge tender, had been a dinner pail boat but now the deckhand had to prepare some meals. His experience as a cook was nil so you can imagine the meals we were served. My home was in Lansingburg in full view of the river. Thanksgiving Day I sailed the *Newark* down river with a tow. My wife waved a towel at me from the front porch. She had a good dinner prepared. The crew and I ate canned beans and frankfurters. A Thanksgiving Day feast!

A week later with the tow safely tied up in Rondout Creek, I was laid off. Along with my pay, I received a nice bonus, which I appreciated, for it was the first I had ever received.

The *Newark* was not as old as some other steamboats that were operating, having been built at Newark, N.J. in 1920, but I still felt that she was in the twilight of her career. There were no real crew quarters as her work did not require them. She had a Buffalo type steering engine in the pilot house which made it uncomfortable hot in the summertime, but the engine handled the big rudder very well. She had good rudder power. Her heavy old wooden hull would lay in the water where it was placed. She was sluggish, but a good handling tug.

The following season the *Newark* was brought out with a single crew under the second captain of the year before. Most of the towing was to be done by the motor launch *Florence*. A young deckhand and I were placed on this vessel as an additional crew. This was a big change for me as I had never even seen a diesel engine.

The *Florence*

The *Florence* was all steel. She was almost new and in very good condition having been built at Manitowac, Wis. in 1936. Her engine was a Kahlenberg semi-diesel of 120 horsepower. She towed very well for her size but could not be compared to a steamboat of the same rated horsepower.

There were three operators on the launch besides myself. None of these had a pilot's license because it was not required on a motor vessel. The first two operators resented me because I had a license. The third operator, Bill Ryan of Troy, welcomed me. He was holding down two jobs, the other being on a launch for NYS DPW. Later he was captain of the *Urger* one of the New York State diesel tugs.

My first day aboard I was shown the engine and told how to operate it. Being semi-diesel, the engine was equipped with glow plugs which were much like cigar lighters. These were switched on when starting the engine to ignite the fuel, then they were switched off when the engine was warmed up. My instructor told me that if one of the cylinders stopped firing when the engine was running the pressure would build up and blow up the cylinder. A glow plug must be turned on before this happened. I was green and believed it. My first few days aboard were miserable because of the worry about the engine. Then I found a manual about the engine operation and everything was okay.

It became prudent for me to make a quick inspection of the engine every time I came on duty. I had found that one or another of the cylinders would frequently stop firing when I started out. When the amount of cooling water to this cylinder was reduced the problem was gone. I made a note of the position of the cooling water valves to all cylinders and reset them to this correct position every time I started a shift.

One day I came to work and found there was a loaded scow ready to be towed to the dump. On the way to get the scow, my deckhand reported water in the bilges and the bilge pump not working. The only way to pump out the hull was with a shaft pump that worked only when the engine was running. The launch was stopped and the pump quickly inspected. A wooden match stick was found in the pump. When this was removed the pump worked properly. We picked up the scow and headed for the dumping area. The deckhand reported the water was again rising in the bilges despite the pump. It was now almost up to the floor plates in the engine room. The scow was placed against the river bank while we searched for the leak. We found no leak but we did find the cause. A valve had been closed in the cooling water discharge line preventing the water from being discharged overboard. Another valve had been opened allowing the water to be discharged into the hull. I reset the valves properly and the shaft pump soon had the bilges emptied. Such annoyances occurred too often to have been accidental. I never reported these happenings. I always reported a dull, uneventful shift. Let him wonder!

The *Florence* was, of course, pilot house controlled. The engine could be started to run in forward or reverse. Normal operation was to start the engine in forward position and select AHEAD or ASTERN by using the big shifting lever. When in ASTERN the backing efficiency was only about forty per cent. Better backing power could be obtained by leaving the lever in the AHEAD and stopping the engine. Thus by restarting the engine in the reverse direction the propeller was reversed and did not lose the power through the clutch.

One afternoon, my deckhand and I were standing on the river bank ready to go to work. The *Florence* came rushing in with five men on the bow deck anxious to get ashore. The operator intended to back down hard to kill the headway and make a flashy landing. He shut the engine off and tried to start it in reverse. It did not start on the first attempt and then it was too late. The little ship stretched half her length up the beach. There was no rail around the bow deck so the men of the dredge crew went flying ashore. The air was full of arms and legs, hats, coats, and lunch boxes. Fortunately, no one was hurt, though the operator was threatened with bodily injury.

The job on the *Florence* was good but there was too much jealousy. The contract was within days of completion when I received another job offer and I left.

Chapter 11

***Winthrop*, Poorhouse Lock 28A, July 1939**

The next three tugs I worked on were owned by Hedger Transportation Company, 120 Wall St., New York City. They were *Winthrop*, built at Wilmington, Del. in 1883; *Dixie*, built at Madison, Md. in 1905; and *Nat Sutton*, built at East Providence, R.I. in 1887. All three were wooden hull steamboats. They had the usual disadvantages of being dirty and cramped for space. When the *Dixie* was light on coal, she would just clear the bridges on the western end of the Erie Canal. I remember going under a railroad bridge and hearing the tick, tick, tick, sound of the pilot house just touching the rivets. That was too close! The *Nat Sutton* was the most powerful of the three. There was no steamboat in the canal that could out perform her with a heavy hawser tow. Her very heavy hand gear made her less desirable for any other type of work. The *Dixie* had a steam steering gear and was the best of these vessels for shifting work. When thinking of the *Winthrop*, I recall the very hot sleeping quarters and the boiler that frequently developed cracks.

Leo Suprenant of Waterford was Master on these ships and I was his Mate. He had just been promoted to Captain and was the last man on the company's list which is why he got the old steamboats, and the men with more seniority got the cleaner diesels. We complimented each other because I had a pilot's license for New York Harbor, which he lacked, and he had Buffalo Harbor, which I lacked at the time.

Winthrop, **Lock # 2, Waterford, NY**

Each of these tugs had an extension for the inside smoke-stack that could be raised up into place by turning a crank in the boiler room. When approaching a bridge this extension would be cranked down and telescoped down in between the inside and outside stack. The firemen liked the added draft it gave to their fires. A small whistle in the fireroom was actuated from the pilot house to notify the firemen to crank the stack down. It was new to me and I frequently forgot to blow the whistle, but the fireman usually had the stack lowered without my signal. A couple of times we both failed to react and the stack was knocked off necessitating some work to put it back. This made me unpopular with the firemen.

The tows for these tugs were made up at the canal terminal at Columbia Street, Brooklyn. Each tow consisted of four "Hedger Boxes," large, wooden, square-ended barges. *Harvest Queen* and *Sulpher King* were the two largest. Most of these barges had high cabins so they had to be loaded at all times in the canal to clear bridges. A barge would often be loaded deeper than it should have been which caused much difficulty in the shallow sections. It was a long heavy drag with these tows up the Hudson River, up the Mohawk River, through the Erie Canal System and up the Niagara River to the canal terminal at Buffalo. The worst drag was over the sixty mile level from Rochester to Lockport. In this narrow, shallow section of the Erie canal, against the current, dragging over the bottom, our speed was at most one mile per hour.

Dixie **entering the head of the "flight of stairs," Waterford, NY**

One afternoon, I was on watch westbound on this stretch of the canal. A boy was hiding in the bushes and shooting at me with a B-B gun. He would take his shots then run ahead to hide in the bushes. When the tug arrived at his position, I would again become his target. I was glad when he finally wearied of the game.

On arrival at Buffalo, the tow landed at the canal terminal at West Genessee Street. The runner for Hedger would be on the pier with a slip of paper containing some shifts to be made around the harbor and then our tow back to New York. There was no let up. It was all slow, heavy work. The days turned into weeks and still the same dull, monotonous work had to be done.

Nat Sutton

Almost all of the barges owned and operated by individuals had disappeared from the canal. There were no children on the company-owned boats although there were some married couples. Tugboat men were envious of the bargeman who had his pretty young wife along with him. There were also the gals that I called "trippers" who came aboard a barge to act as cook or companion for one trip or more. I don't know the reasons for their actions. It might have been a spirit of adventure of just a chance for someone down on her luck and hungry to get three meals a day. A young woman in Buffalo, who wanted to get to The Big Apple, asked a middle aged bargeman if she could ride his boat to New York. He readily agreed. Men on the fleet stood a two hour watch on the wheel helping to steer the tow when in the canal. The steering wheel was on the bow of the second boat and the obliging barge captain's boat was third in the tow. When he stood a trick at the wheel his passenger was locked in the cabin so the other men on the fleet could not become acquainted with her.

It was aggravating to be stuck aboard ship on a beautiful day and see other people enjoying themselves. We would watch the yachtsmen and their guests, the couples in canoes, the families on bathing beaches, and the picnicers along the shore. It might have been Saturday, or Sunday, or a holiday, but it meant nothing to the tugboat crew. To them it was just another day and a time of envy and sometimes despair.

The only time available to go home was when the tow went through "The Flight." The double locking took some time to accomplish, so I would sometimes manage an hour or two at home. The captain did not want to work any system between us to allow extra hours off. My son George was born in 1939 while I was on this job. I managed to get off the day after the birth for six or eight hours. Jobs were scarce so I stuck it out, waiting for the winter lay up.

The deckhand had a poor job. At every lock the hawsers had to be shortened which meant that the deckhand off watch had to be rousted out to help. His short time alotted to sleep would be broken up. The pilot would tell the deckie on watch to call his helper to pull hawser. If the man did not come out quickly, he would be called much earlier the next time and have to stand around and wait. This would get him wide awake and spoil his sleep. After a few times, the man off watch would jump out of the bunk, immediately pull his hawser, and jump back in the bunk. It would take only minutes and he would quickly be asleep again. Sometimes I think they never fully woke up.

Neither the captain nor I used the searchlight very much. It was considered demeaning to be known as a "searchlight pilot." We would go many nights without ever using it. Searchlights could not be atop the pilot house because of the low bridges. The one on the *Winthrop* was on the stem head and awkward to use.

Nat Sutton locking down with first pair of barges. Note stern of tug outside of barge corner to make more toom.

Nat Sutton below lock, waiting for second locking. Note barges, built of concrete in WWI, were sunk and piers built in them to make approach wall to lock.

Some of the bargemen complained about suddenly finding the tow entering a guard gate that they had not expected. After that we always illuminated the guard gates and the narrow bridges for the wheelsman on the tow. These fleets could not be steered as could a fleet of canal boats. The steersman could hold the tow steady or even help the tug to turn it. He could not turn the tow against the pull of the tug. Several men were injured trying to do this.

Running without using a searchlight provided us with some amusement. There was one section of the sixty mile level we called "The Flume." It was a popular Lover's Lane and cars were parked under the trees on the canal bank. These three tugs all had compound engines and no exterior exhaust so they were very quiet. The car's occupants would not notice the tug approach until they were suddenly bathed in the bright light from the spotlight. Some of them waved at us, some of them ignored us, and some became very angry. Tugs pushing barges were denied this amusement because the searchlights were needed to see, thus the lovers were alerted. Another advantage we had over push tows was the ability to run in fog. The pushers had to see so far ahead of the pilot house that they needed lights. In the fog, the light reflected back and blinded the pilot. The man with a hawser tow did not need to see so far ahead. In a land cut, his deck lights would illuminate the canal bank on each side and allow him to stay in the middle. His vision ahead was very limited. He had to be aware that he might suddenly come upon a push tow stopped in the fog.

High water in the Mohawk was sometimes a problem. We had an eastbound tow consisting of three "boxes" and two barge canal boats. The two small boats were loaded with pig iron. Because of its great weight in the bottom of the barge, a great strain is placed on the sides. This is hard on a good barge and worse on an old one. We had been told that these two old boats were to be discarded after this trip. About ten p.m. when between Lock #18 and #17, the first watch experienced a very heavy rainfall for a few minutes. They proceeded into Lock #17 with no difficulty. I came on watch at midnight leaving the lock. The locktender had said that the river was beginning to rise. After leaving the lock it was apparent that the current was increasing rapidly. About half way over the level, we went around a bend and there was a dredge in the channel with a half-loaded dump scow alongside. I got the tug and first two boxes past the dredge, but the third one hit the scow and broke it loose from the dredge. The dredge-tending launch caught the scow downstream and tied it up to a tree. I was sorry to have hit the scow, but it could have been worse. If either of the small canal boats had hit anything they would have dropped right there.

I was relieved when I got the tow into the land cut and out of the river current. When I arrived at Mindenville Guard Gate, I turned on the seardchlight for the bargemen. Imagine my surprise to find that the bottom of the gate was about even with the pilot house windows. Quick action was called for. There was no time to stop the tow. I backed the tug to port and stopped the engine so the water would not be stirred up any more. The bargeman threw the hawsers off and they were pulled in. He then steadied the tow through the guard gate. Our tow went drifting down the canal and we were on the opposite side of the gate. Later in the morning the flood gates on the dam were opened. By afternoon the water level was lowered enough for us to get under the gate. We picked up the tow and took it to Lock #16 where we tied up.

Our tow was not harmed but the dump scow did suffer some damage. The dredge was the D.D.#4 that I had worked on and I was surprised to find that the dredge crew was the same crew I had worked with. The men came to the lock to visit me and we had some good natured joking. They claimed that the water came up so fast that they were unable to move out of the channel. It was a real cloudburst. The dredge company brought suit for damages but lost the case.

I finished the 1939 season with Hedger and then took the winter off. There was no unemployment insurance then for sailors. The pay checks had to be banked in the summer to be sure of eating in the winter. The following spring the employment situation was no better so I returned to work on the same job. I hated it, but I didn't dare quit. There were many good men walking the docks looking for work. Every chance I got I looked for a steering job somewhere else. Midway in the season, I got fed up and suddenly walked away from the boat. It was a risky move but it turned out well. Four days later, I had a far better position. The *Nat Sutton* was my last steam powered vessel.

My hatred of this type of towboat work does not mean that the company had any shortage of men. There were many of them with long years of service with the company.

Changes in the transportation industry soon finished off Hedger.

Lester Eckert and Herbert Lake, deckhands, 1940

Otco coated with ice returning from Philadelphia.

Otco with two light barges on Long Island Sound, Dec. 25, 1940.

Chapter 12

The next tugboat that I became acquainted with was the *Otco* owned by Oil Transfer Corp. What a change! Up until now I had been working on aging steamboats, but the *Otco* was a new, modern all steel diesel tug, built at Brooklyn, N.Y. in 1938. The quarters were luxurious compared to others. There was ample room even with three crews aboard. The Captain and the Chief Engineer each had a room to himself, the mates had a two bunk stateroom as did the asst. engineers, the unlicensed men were accommodated in a roomy well-furnished fo'csle. Each room had a sink with hot and cold running water, a medicine cabinet, good mattresses, and white bed linen. The crew was also supplied with bath towels and hand towels. This marked a change in the tugboat era. Up until this time all tugs I had known were furnished with blue bed linen and no towels. From this time forward I found all tugs furnished white bed linen and towels for the crew.

The ship was well insulated against the summer heat and a good system provided steam heat to all areas in winter. Two shower rooms with flush toilets were located one on each side. The well-equipped galley was aft. All areas of the ship were accessible from any other area without going outside nor going through anyone's stateroom. She was the best designed tug of her size for the crew's comfort that I ever knew.

I was offered the position of second mate on the *Otco* over the telephone by the company's New York office. Ralph Matton, of John E. Matton & Son, had recommended me to them. The *Otco* was working on Lakes Erie and Ontario. My statement that I had never worked on the Great Lakes was brushed aside and I was told to meet the tug at Oswego. The towboat companies were now operating their tugs with three crews when on the Great

Lakes. They were afraid the Coast Guard would give them trouble if only two crews were aboard.

When the *Otco* arrived at Oswego I introduced myself to her Master, Cal Derrickson of Philadelphia, Pa. He also brushed aside my statement that I had never worked on the Great Lakes. We left Oswego with the loaded barge. The lake was just rough enough so that the tug could not stay behind the barge so the sea hawser was stretched out. My watch was to be 12 to 4, and being tired from traveling, I crawled into my bunk. At midnight, I reported to the wheelhouse. The skipper gave me the compass course he was steering and left with the remark that he would see me at breakfast. There I was on a strange ship, with an unknown crew, on a dark night, on Lake Erie, a body of water of which I had no knowledge. I tooted for the deckhand and put him on the wheel. After checking the log for our last known position I pulled out the chart for Lake Erie. Satisfying myself that all was as it should be, I settled down to the short four hour watch. Some weeks later I told Cal that it was not a good idea to turn the ship over to an unknown greenhorn like that. He replied that I had been well checked out before I was offered the job. We soon developed a mutual liking and respect for each other.

The pilot house was well equipped with an accurate compass, a radio direction finder, and a powerful radio telephone. There was a good chart table with an ample supply of charts. The windows were of heavy plate glass and operated with a crank. Steel shutters were on hand to cover them in a storm but were never used while I was there. Sea water alone would not break those windows. Many times I saw solid green water over them and they didn't even leak.

Work on the lakes with three crews aboard was a great change for me. Shifts of four hours on and eight hours off seemed like no work at all. If we were towing on a hawser I would steer the first and last hours of my watch and have the deckhand steer the middle two. I was bored by this dull steering on a compass course. Most pilots liked it as being easy and without the chance of doing damage. I was in the minority. I liked short work and enjoyed shifting, such as around the piers in New York. On the late night watches, I used to talk on the ship-to-ship frequencies of the radio telephone with men on other vessels. I regularly contacted the Blue Line steam tugs *Spartan* and *Sachem* in Long Island Sound and the Connecticut River.

Blue Line tug *Sachem* on Connecticut River

Because of the weather we were confined to the cabin much of the time and seldom went on deck. Reading was a popular pastime. Card playing was enjoyed by many of us. Small stakes poker was played but Red Dog was the usual game. This often developed into a rather expensive pastime for some. I was lucky and made all my spending money at this game. When Lady Luck turned against me and finances were low, I would get into a game of Hearts. The skipper was good at Red Dog but a weak Hearts player. I usually managed to make a little stake and get back into the bigger game.

Hand laundry was not something I enjoyed doing so I used the laundry at Buffalo. Whenever we entered Buffalo Harbor the little steam launch would come alongside and pick up all of the ship's dirty linen. They also handled personal laundry for the crew members so I gave them my dirty clothes to launder. In about two hours, the laundry was back. My clothes were all washed and pressed and my khakis stiffly starched. Included was a nice laundry bag for future use. My name and the ship's name had been neatly embroidered on it. From that time on I just tossed the bag and its contents into the launch when it came alongside.

The First Mate was a young man from Detroit named Eastman. He was licensed as Master of Oceans, had a lot of pilotage, and was constantly studying. As a navigator he was excellent, as a tugboat handler not as good. We were on a run to a terminal far up Cuyahoga Creek at Cleveland, Ohio. The bridges gave us a lot of trouble when they waited a long time before opening. It was not bad going in with the loaded barge, but coming out was another matter. We towed the light barge out on short stern lines. If we could keep moving it was fine, but if stopped it was very hard to stay in shape. One bridge always held us up and this was Eastman's undoing. He invariably wound up with the rake of the barge on top of the tug knocking down the pipe rail on the boat deck. The Skipper told me not to turn the wheel over to him if we were coming out of this area until we cleared the bridge. I told him that I would gladly do the job but I was not about to refuse to turn the watch over to the First Mate. Apparently the Skipper did not want to tell him either so we continued as before. It is not surprising that Eastman had trouble. The *Otco* was fine when strapped to a barge, but when light she was a terrible ship to handle. I had found that a wooden hull tugboat would stay in place in the water much better than a steel hull. The *Otco* was steel and also shallow in the bow. The least bit of water hitting the bow would start her spinning around. The usual way to turn a tug around was to go ahead with the rudder hard right. When it became necessary to go into reverse the tug's stern would back to port thus maintaining the turn. This did not work with the *Otco*. One could never predict which way that light bow was going to swing. The best way to turn was to back up first. This would start the bow swinging. That was the direction to make the turn. The Chief used to say that we gave him more bells, and thus more work, when landing the light tug than when landing a barge. The First Mate was a friendly personable, well trained young man with a good license. His experience had been on big ships and not on tugboats. He was not a tug handler.

Sometime later, I heard that he was Steamboat Inspector in the Coast Guard at Detroit.

Cal Derrickson, the Captain, had only a license for pilot in the New York State Canal System but he had much more pilot knowledge than that. He would confidently take his ship anywhere it was sent whether he had been there before or not. We used to say that if he were given orders to go to France he would go. Not having any knowledge of celestial navigation, he would head east until he made a landfall. Then he would go ashore, find out where he was, buy some charts, and continue on. Rough weather did not stop him. He used to say with his Southern drawl "the *Otco* is like a can buoy. When you button her up, the water can't get in except down her smokestack." She survived a lot of rough weather, but gave her crew quite a ride.

There were three of us in her crew who did not enjoy the wild antics of the tug when the water got lumpy. The second assistant, the oiler and I all suffered from sea sickness. I was embarrassed by it but the skipper said he had been the same way and had gotten over it. He predicted that I would gradually be less affected by it and would soon be completely cured. He was partially right. I improved to the point where Cal remarked that I was cured. Wishful thinking! On the last trip of the season, I was violently ill. Anti-seasick pills were used by many men engaged in this type of work with varying results. They did not help me. There were other tugboat men including several captains, who suffered from this embarrassing malady. Most of them, like me, avoided work on the lakes when possible.

The little *Otco* saw here share of rough water that fall. One afternoon we had a light barge on hawser running into a head sea. A loaded 600 ft. ore carrier was going in the opposite direction. The swells were running along her sides from stern to bow but because of her length and weight she seemed as steady as a pool table. One of her sailors called his shipmates to look at us. They were pointing and laughing at us. The *Otco* was pounding up and down throwing spray in all directions. They probably could look right under our bow at times. Such is life on small ships.

One rough trip we brought our loaded barge into port and found it was down by the head. On inspection, we found that a weld in her bow had cracked open. The bargemen were unhappy. They had been unable to get out of their cabin or have a fire in the galley stove because of the water washing over the cabin.

There was one time when the Coast Guard thought we might have gone down. We left Cleveland just before midnight with a light barge stretched out on half of the length of the sea hawser. Storm warnings had just been hoisted up. I came on watch and suggested to Cal that we put out the rest of the hawser. He said not to put it out without his permission. A half hour later, with the sea building up rapidly, I sent the deckhand down to the skipper with the same suggestion and got the same reply. Shortly after this the captain came into the pilot house and said we had better put the rest of the hawser out. It was a little bit too late. The sea had swept over our stern and turned half of the coiled hawser over upon itself. Now it was tangled. Cal stayed in the wheel house and kept the tug on course. I went to the after steering station on the boat deck to control the engine speed and supervise the three deckhands. They were working with seawater swirling around them and had to be careful. If one of them went over the side, we might not be able to pick him up. We finally managed to get most of the long hawser stretched out leaving us with a snarl of manila rope on the stern deck.

The skipper was trying to make up his mind between going on and returning to Cleveland. He decided to ask the Coast Guard at Cleveland what the wind direction and velocity was. He called them on 2182 kc. a few times with no answer. Whether from disgust or some other reason, he snapped off the radiophone even though we both knew we should keep a watch on 2182 kc. The decision was made to head back for Cleveland so the next problem was turning around. At some point we would be broadside to the sea with the light barge yanking on our hawser. We waited for what looked like a good opportunity and made the turn successfully. It was now about 0330. The First Mate came in and remarked that he had been thrown out of bed and sleep was impossible. He said it was almost time for him to go on watch so if I didn't feel well he would relieve me. I had been too busy to think of sea sickness but now that it was suggested, my stomach became queasy. I turned the watch over to him and went to visit the head.

We finally got back to Cleveland and anchored the barge behind the breakwater about 0900. The tug went in to a dock and tied up. A Coast Guard officer came aboard and asked what our trouble was. It seems that the radio station at Lorain, Ohio had heard us calling the Coast Guard on 2182 kc. with no answer. Lorain knew that the Coast Guard did not monitor that frequency so they alerted them that we were calling. After repeated calls for the *Otco* from Cleveland Coast Guard were not answered they thought perhaps we had gone down in the storm. when we reappeared in their harbor an officer was sent to question us. I don't remember what excuse the Captain made for not answering the radio call. Perhaps he said the rig was malfunctioning.

On the last trip of the season, we were told that we had just enough time to get back to Oswego before the canal closed for the winter if we lost no time for weather. We made entrance into the canal in time but not without a rough ride. The first mate and one crew were discharged at Oswego and we proceeded to New York.

My daughter, Patricia, was born when I was on the *Otco* on Lake Erie. She was two weeks old when I met her.

That year was the only time I worked on Christmas Day. The tug was tied up for some minor repairs and maintenance. I had a few days home to get reacquainted with my family. The tug was coming out at midnight on Christmas Eve so we had our little Christmas celebration December 24th. The tug had to work because we had a contract to lighten an ocean going oil tanker at New London, Conn. and she came in on Christmas Day. We took two light barges to the job and, along with other tugs and barges, carried the oil cargo from New London back to the Connecticut River and up to Hartford.

Much of our work that winter was oil barges from The Kills in New Jersey to oil docks in the Connecticut River. This river freezes in winter. The *Otco* was a good ice breaker. Though rated only 720 horse power she had it all. When trimmed light in the bow, she could break a lot of ice but the crew did not get much sleep because of the noise.

Late in the winter we towed a light barge to Philadelphia to load for Atlantic City. While the barge was loading, a man came aboard the tug and introduced himself. He was master of a tug or tanker which was owned by the oil company that we were doing this job for. He was going to ride with us to become acquainted with Atlantic City. The weather turned bad so the barge was anchored at Lewes, Del. to await better weather. We stayed there two days during which time our visitor changed his mind and went ashore. Perhaps he found out that none of us had ever been into Atlantic City. When the weather improved, we proceeded on and were met outside of Atlantic City about 10 p.m. by the little pilot boat. No pilot came aboard but he ran slow ahead of us and guided us into the harbor. We were in radiophone contact with him all the time. We pulled the hawser and picked up the barge alongside. The pilot put his spotlight on the dock we wanted and left. The barge was landed with no difficulty. We made one more trip on this run without the use of a pilot.

When we returned to New York, the *Otco* was put in the shipyard for annual overhaul. The boss told me to report to one of their other tugs but I told him I wanted to go home for a while. He said that I was to report "or else." I said I would be right up for my check. When I got to the office, he said that he had been talking to the tug captain. Cal wanted to keep me, so I could go home for a while. My reply was that I was sorry but I had met another tugboat captain while crossing Battery Park and had agreed to take a job as mate with him in two weeks. The boss was a little upset with me.

The *Otco* was a well equipped, well maintained ship with comfortable quarters for the crew. She was suitable for the work she was required to do. Her low pilot house and poor handling qualities would make her undesirable for general harbor work.

Chapter 13

In "The Flight" pushing Blue Line # 103.

While walking through Battery Park late in the winter of 1940, I met my uncle Fred H. Godfrey. He asked me if I needed job and I replied that the offer came at just the right time as I had just quit. The *Thomas A. Feeney* was coming out in two weeks with Fred as Master and I agreed to act as his mate. This tug was owned by Reliance Marine Corp. of Kingston but was under bare boat charter to James McWilliams Blue Line Inc.

The *Thomas A. Feeney* was a conversion of the steam tug *Socony 6* which had been built at Philadelphia, Pa. in 1896. She had a steel hull with deck and house of wood. Her engine was a 450 horsepower Fairbanks - Morse diesel. It was intended that she would do canal work but the pilot house was built too low for pushing oil barges. A removable lazy board was installed at the level of the pilot house windows and a hole was cut in the roof. A small shelter with fold out windows was built over this hole. We used this a couple of years but it was awkward. It was also poorly heated. We complained to Bernie Feeney about this at every opportunity. Blue Line also mentioned it to him. He finally capitulated and had his carpenters build a higher, roomier pilot house. A new radiator was also made up. It covered the whole area under the front windows from the sills to the deck and from door to door. It was a big one and had no valve to shut it off. Bernie told us he hoped it would roast us. He wanted no more complaints about lack of heat.

Reliance Marine had operated this tug for several years but they had bad luck and an excessive amount of damage. The Feeney boys decided it would be easier to charter her out as a bare boat and let someone else have the headaches. We worked several years with good luck and a minimum amount of damage so Feeney was encouraged. Two more small tugs were purchased. When the *Thomas* was released from charter they kept Fred on as Master and operated a fleet of three tugs. That company treated me very well. Although I was working for Blue Line, I received a bonus each Christmas from Feeney.

Our first work that summer was pushing the Blue Line #103 with oil products from The Kills to Rochester and other Erie Canal ports. The *Thomas A. Feeney* did not have the high horse-power of the new tugs that had been built in recent years but she did well enough at canal work. Her steering engine was an adaptation of a large heavy duty air drill that handled the big rudder very well.

We were operating with two crews. The Chief Engineer was Bill McGowan and the Assistant Engineer was George Jordan, both of Kingston. The union had obtained three crews for the harbor boats so they could rotate the crews with two aboard ship and one always at home. The canal tugs had received wage increases and other benefits, but still had only two crews. The captain and I cooperated with each other in order to get home occasionally. One would steer both watches for 24 to 48 hours and let the other go home. Twenty-four hours on watch became an easy chore but after that it became more difficult. The second night watch was hard on the eyes. Coffee consumption was very high; dousing cold water on ones face helped for only a short time; walking back and forth in the pilot house helped. Who ever heard of a person falling asleep while walking? It was tempting the Sand Man to sit on the pilot's chair and relax. I used to hope we would be delayed at a lock by a double locking so that I could sleep twenty minutes or so. A nap of about five minutes could be managed in each lock if sleep came immediately after stopping. After such a short snooze, I generally felt worse for a few minutes, but then felt refreshed. Thick fog was welcomed, especially if it came when we were near a good place to tie up. That meant a full refreshing sleep. Light or intermittent fog was the worst thing that could happen for the eyes then became more and more tired. Many times, when relieved after a long shift, sleep would not come. Eyes abused by too much use and a stomach quivering from too much coffee would prohibit relaxation for a time. The longest time I worked alone was four days and three nights. Fred went home from New York and I worked alone for twenty-four hours in the harbor. (We had not known this was going to happen.) I then picked up the Blue Line #103 at Bayway and headed for the canal. After an exhausting trip I was relieved at Rome, N.Y. Harsh words were exchanged between the captain and me because of this. We normally got on well together but when he went ashore I never knew when he would be back.

Our deckhands were Tommy McGowan, who had some experience, and young lad from Rensselaer named Eddie, who was on a tug for the first time. They were good boys, but not much help to the man who was in the pilot house with no relief.

One of the deckhand's regular chores is carrying coffee to the pilot on watch. Our skipper always said that he wanted exactly two drops of milk in his coffee mug. One night Eddie very carefully put *three* drops of evaporated milk in a cup of coffee which he handed to Fred in the dark pilot house. For whatever reason, Fred chose this moment to be critical and say "You put too damn much milk in this coffee." Eddie was flabbergasted! His skipper could tell the difference between two and three drops of milk in a cup of coffee.

This reminds me of a story my father used to tell about a green deckhand he had. My dad was steering a tug with a hawser tow on the straight Rome level. Tug and tow were running nice and steady. He tooted for the deckhand, called him to the pilot house, and told him to "watch her." Dad went to the head and, sitting there with the door open, he noticed the tug getting closer and closer to the shore. Hurriedly yanking up his trousers, he ran to the pilot house and pulled the wheel over. The deckhand was very excited and apologetic. "Don't blame me George," he said. "I did just what you said. I watched her. I never touched the wheel."

We had a pleasant summer in the Canal. One of our pastimes on hot summer afternoons was what we called aquaplaning. A heaving line tied to the first bitt forward on the barge would extend about 3/4 of the barge length back to a sheet of plywood about 3' by 5'. One could stand on this sheet of wood and glide on top of the water. By tipping it a little it could be made to go out away from the barge. A ladder was fastened to the last bitt aft on the barge and extending into the water. Anyone who fell off had to swim quickly to get to the ladder before it was too late.

Author and Tommy McGowan, 1941.

One day we were in Arthur Kill and enjoying ourselves in this fashion when we heard a great burst of cheering. We were passing the Elizabethport, N.J. Recreation Pier and had a large audience. They thought the show was put on for them but we had not even realized they were there. It was not often that we did this anywhere but in the narrow sections of the canal.

A couple of trips on Lake Erie convinced the office that this tug was too slow for this work. It was just as well because we would have to be very careful and avoid bad weather which would cause some lost time. The *Thomas A. Feeney* might not survive in a big storm.

Sun Oil, Cleveland, Ohio, June 10, 1941

Occasionally we made a trip down Long Island Sound to New Haven or Hartford. This was nice in the summer as it was always cool and pleasant. When in the Connecticut River, we took a pilot aboard. One day, when bound down river with a light oil barge on stern lines, we had some excitement. The pilot yelled "get away." I looked out and saw a canoe headed directly for the side of the tug. The two men in the canoe saw that they could not make it and they stopped paddling but did not try to steer away nor stop. The canoe missed the tug and went broadside under the rake of the barge. The men each put a hand up against the bow and the canoe and contents rolled under the barge. I told the pilot to turn around and go back but he said there was not room enough to turn. I relieved him and turned the tow around and went back. The two men were holding onto the submerged canoe and paddling toward shore. They said they were all right but had lost a camera. They were lucky not to have lost much more than that, possibly their lives.

We made a lot of trips to West Haven, Connecticut. Occasionally we were given a tow of coal barges but this work was too heavy for the little tug. When the tide in Long Island Sound turned against us we could barely make headway. One night we were bucking tide with a tow of wooden coal boats about one mile from New Haven breakwater when the wind freshened up from the southeast. The water was rolling up onto the decks of the barges and some spray going into the open hatches. One bargeman could not start his gasoline pump. It took us a so long to travel that mile that the barge took on a quantity of water. We finally made it into the harbor to the stake boat, but the coal boat finally sank.

Blue Line was a good outfit to work for and Bill Garrett, the Old Sarge of WWI, was a good boss. He sounded rough and tough but he was fair and cared for the men. I had two harsh arguments with him in nine years time. One of these I won and one was a draw. As soon as the argument was over he was his usual self, holding no grudge. In fact, I believe he respected someone who stood up for what was thought to be right. Many times, on Sunday morning, he told us that he could spare us for a couple of hours if we wanted to go to church. Several times, in the cold of winter, he allowed me to stop at Pier #6 East River and go to the Seaman's Church Institute on South Street for a good hot shower. His only admonition was to hurry it up and to phone the office immediately after. There should have been more bosses like him.

The union had now obtained an eight hour day for all the tugs and the men could have some regular time home. One system used was twenty twelve hour days aboard ship and ten days home without pay; others worked two weeks on and one week off. Men working closer to home used other shorter systems. Some greedy men worked all the time that they could with little or no time off. There was plenty of work for all.

One spring season we had a problem with high water. After delivering a load of oil to a terminal in Rochester we headed back east. Some time had been lost on the way up because of high water, and constant rain had made conditions worse. Flood conditions forced us to tie up at Lock #25. The water continued to rise and the lock walls were soon under water. Three or four weeks were spent tied up while the water receded very slowly. Several units were tied up there and some crews were laid off. Blue Line was good to their men and we were kept on the payroll. As the water level dropped I was anxious to get under way again. Time passed rather slowly out there in the boondocks and I also wanted to repay the company for treating us so well. The level was still very high, but I felt that it could be navigated safely if we could get under the bridge at Weedsport. A car was hired to take me to the bridge which I measured with a steel tape borrowed from the bargeman. The clearance was far less than what was required for the tug. Determined to go if possible, we filled the bow tank with water. Cables were placed on the stern bitts of the barge and led under her bottom to come up at the center of her stern. Ratchets connected these cables to the stem head of the tug. When the ratchets were fully tightened it pulled the bow of the tug down, but still not enough to clear the bridge. All of the pushing cables were tightened up and the bilges under the engine room and pump room of the barge were flooded. This caused the stern of the barge to sink deeper in the water and pull the bow of the tug down also. Measurement of the pilot house showed we should have two inches clearance. We now had another problem. The stern was so high out of water that we would lose some rudder power. This could be corrected as soon as we cleared the bridge by reversing our previous actions. A small flagstaff on the upper deck aft was now too high to clear the bridge so we sawed it off and got underway. We approached the bridge "hooked up" and I stepped out of the wheelhouse onto the bow deck just in case we didn't clear. All went well and once we passed Three River Point, conditions became much better.

The war in Europe caused a great change in our work. Tugs, barges, and all types of vessels were in short supply. Some small diesel tugs like the *Robin Hood* had already been purchased, put on the decks of ships, and taken somewhere overseas. After our entry into the war some tugs and oil barges were confiscated by Uncle Sam. My company lost the Blue Line #102 to this program. I later saw a picture in Life Magazine showing the barge in Greenland. Later in the war the government confiscated many oil barges and railroad carfloats to be used in the invasion of France. These barges were stripped of everything on deck and of all equipment so that they became merely steel scows. The Blue Line #103 was taken for this purpose. After the war all scows that remained were towed back to New York. Bill Garrett asked me if I could pick out the Blue Line #103 now that she was merely an empty steel can. I thought I could identify her by the bitts, cleats, her skegs, and perhaps some of the old dents in her hull. This proved to be the case. Blue Line purchased the scow and had it refitted as an oil barge. She was given her old name of Blue Line #103 and was used for many more years.

The movement of gasoline decreased considerably because of rationing, but we still had some canal work. It was a pleasure to get away from the hectic harbor work once in a while. Bernie Feeney had placed one of his painters aboard so that the tug would be painted sooner and would look well. The man was a mild- mannered little German. He made no impression on us at first but then came a change. One evening we were in the canal about one hour from our destination when the deckhand came up to tell me that this painter was in the galley doing card tricks for the crew. They all knew that I was an avid card player. As soon as we tied up I went down to the galley. The painter fanned a deck of cards out toward me and said to take any one and show it to the boys. I did as I was told and received a big laugh. He had told them which card I would take before I came down. The tricks he did were amazing. He could deal out poker hands where two of them were very good but his was always better. I watched him very closely but could not detect any irregularity in his deal. He said he had paid his way through school by gambling on the trains in Europe and sometimes on the transAtlantic steamers. Why was a man of his education and talent working as a painter for low wages? I wish I had asked him.

We were put to work, along with many other units, hauling crude oil from Frontier Fuel in Tonawanda to plants in "The Kills." It seemed strange to be loaded eastbound and in ballast westbound. The barges would pump their water ballast ashore at Frontier Fuel and then load the oil barge. Frequently several units would be at the terminal at the same time thus causing long delays. To save time some of the barge captains discharged the ballast into the Niagara River while waiting for a berth. They could open some valves and let the water go out by gravity, which was rather slow. They could also pump it out through the seacock so that it was not visible to anyone watching. One night we were awaiting a berth and the bargeman was pumping ballast through the seacock when a small U.S. Coast Guard patrol boat came alongside. The uniformed men came aboard the barge and exchanged pleasantries with the barge captain and then came to the tug for coffee. The men on the barge thought sure that they were in trouble for contaminating the river. The engines and pumps on the barge were running full blast with the usual noise and the clattering and banging noises that accompanied this operation. If the pumps were stopped it would call attention to the fact that they had been pumping. The barge was getting higher and higher out of the water. Apparently these young men knew nothing about oil barges and as long as no water was being discharged from the hose everything was okay. The bargemen were very much relieved when the Coast Guard craft finally left.

Some difficulty was experienced on the sixty mile level when meeting other oil barges or loaded tows. The channel was so narrow that often each tow would be aground on their starboard side while their port sides would be touching. Sometimes one unit would back up to a place that might be a little wider. When both units were stuck and unable to move there was nothing to do but wait. In very rare instances another tug would come along and render assistance. Most often, after two or three hours of waiting, the two tows would wriggle past each other. The wide barges in the narrow canal had acted as a dam and caused the water level to rise a little bit.

Another change in canal traffic was the LCTs being brought down from Tonawanda to New York City. These landing craft for tanks were built for the U.S. Navy and had new inexperienced crews aboard. They should not be criticized for their lack of knowledge for they had probably enlisted only a few weeks earlier. These shallow draft, multi-engined vessels should have been easy to control but had a lot of trouble. They ran aground, crashed into lock walls, guard gates, and other vessels. These troubles ceased when the navy hired some tugboat men to pilot them to New York when on their time off.

New York Harbor lost its glitter and glamour during the war. It no longer was the port that was lighted up like a Christmas tree. The glow from the city had silhouetted the ships off our east coast and made them sitting ducks for enemy submarines so the "brown out" was put into effect. It was not a complete blackout, but was an attempt to remedy the situation. The buildings had lighting restrictions placed on them. Many lighted buoys were extinguished and others decreased in candlepower as were the lighthouses and beacons.

No weather reports were broadcast and we were forbidden to discuss the weather over the radiophone. All self-propelled vessels had to carry code flags and display the code of the day when passing through The Narrows or past Throggs Neck. We were told to watch for other vessels and aircraft that might flash Morse code signals to us at night. A whole list of two and three letter codes was given to us. The only one I now remember was O S. This translated to "heave to or I will open fire upon you." We were also told that in the event of a blackout of the city we were to extinguish all our lights and anchor until the blackout was over. I think it would have been a grave mistake to completely darken ship in a harbor as busy as New York was during wartime.

Blue Line lent the *Thomas A. Feeney* to McAllister Brothers for a few weeks and we became involved in a different type of work. We towed scows loaded with copper bars from two different copper docks in Arthur Kill to piers in the North River, probably to go aboard some ship. These copper bars were valuable but there was no guard on the scows. Double pay was received when towing ammunition but we had only one tow of this kind for about two hours. The double pay jobs were reserved for McAllister's own men. When ships loaded ammunition from scows a tug would stand by. The ship would be anchored with an ammunition scow alongside and the tug would hang off the stern of the ship on a long line. We did not get any of this easy duty for double pay.

A couple of trips were made from Port Newark with planes going to Floyd Bennett Field in Jamaica Bay. Someone told me that they were Martin Bombers. Two of these twin-engined airships were loaded on each deckscow. They had been wrapped in a cocoon of black material to protect them from the elements. That was the way they were protected when they were shipped to England on the decks of ships. After we delivered these planes they were to be removed from the protective covering and serviced to be flown across the Atlantic.

A Merritt & Chapman derrick was towed to Floyd Bennett Field by a McAllister tug. The *Thomas A. Feeney* picked up the loaded scows at Port Newark and towed them to this derrick. The planes were lifted ashore and the scows and derrick brought back to the harbor.

As a protection against submarines New York Bay below The Narrows was sown with mines. An anti-submarine net was stretched from Norton Point across the bay. A navy vessel acted as net tender and opened a gate in the net to let any properly identified vessels pass thorough. When we approached this area, with our code flags flying, we would be hailed again and again by officious little Coast Guard boats. They would question us as to our destination and wanted to be sure that we were in the clear channel through the mine field.

One day we were sent to get a derrick boat out of Coney Island Creek. We went through The Narrows hoping for a patrol boat to show us how to get to our destination safely. None appeared. We edged along down the bay and suddenly the deck-hand said he saw mines alongside of us under the surface. No one else had seen them but we decided that we had better try to retrace our track out of there. Just then a small patrol craft appeared. We asked for help and were led safely to the creek. The man on the patrol boat said we were in no danger because the mines did not detonate on contact but were set off from the shore. We wondered what would happen if our propeller hit one.

Blue Line's coal work had increased. Old barges that had been discarded were repaired and put back into service. Some of them were not in very good condition. The steam tug *Salutation* had a steady run from South Amboy to New Haven with coal barges. The other steamboats also helped on this run and also towed coal to Stamford, Bridgeport, and Hartford. The *Thomas A. Feeney* occasionally had a coal tow but she had neither the weight nor the wallop for this work.

Early in the war the German U boats were sinking ships right outside of New York Harbor. To counter this, the ships avoided this area. They began coming in through Long Island Sound and through Hell Gate. While waiting for slack water the ships would anchor near Stepping Stone Lighthouse. On a dark night, with a hawser tow, it was difficult to find a route between them and not drape the tow around some ship's anchor chain. The pilots on these ships liked to transit Hell Gate on the first or the last of the tide when the current was not strong. As a consequence the tugs went through on the strength of the tide to avoid meeting the ships. In a short time the Hell Gate Pilots began moving the ships at any stage of the tide. I am sure that there were some exciting moments and a few close calls between tows and ships meeting in Hell Gate. I don't remember any accidents.

Some Coast Guard bureaucrat, in his inninite wisdom, came up with a solution to this problem. Traffic lights were installed on the bridge. These were red, amber, and green flashing lights shining up and down the East River. They were meant to control the flow of shipping through this area. It was never explained how a tug and heavy tow, bound out toward the Gate, could stop if the light turned red. It was impossible. The operator of those lights was not always alert. I have run against the red light and met no one, and with the green light, have met other traffic.

When ships were loaded and waiting for a convoy they were anchored in the North River, often as far north as Yonkers. When the convoy was forming these ships would come sailing down across the Upper Bay. They were blacked out except for the navigation lights and were difficult to distinguish at a distance. Many a heavy laden tugboat had a hair-raising time crossing through this stream of ships to get to the East River.

A shortage of men existed. We could get cooks and deckhands from the Merchant Marine training schools. They came complete with uniforms but not much else. The cooks had been taught how to cook for a hundred men but had no idea of what to do for seven. The sailors were completely lost on a tug and had to be trained. Pilot house personnel was very scarce. We were fortunate to have three men. We were frozen in our jobs so we didn't worry about anyone quitting. Our problem was the second mate who was really not qualified to work in the busy harbor. After many near collisions and other problems the crew lost all confidence in him and became very jittery. If he rang a bell to the engine room the whole crew was instantly awake. The control stand for the engine was right by a door on the port side. The engineer would take a quick look around to see if everything was okay. The pilot on the port side forward and the deckhand or cook on the port side aft would look out the door toward the engineer. If there was no danger he told them to go back to bed. Meantime the engineer off watch would open the door from his room into the engine room to receive the same reassurance. The mate also needed help doing his work. After seven days on with him I was very tired and glad to see my relief, as he also was to see me. We were willing to put up with this inconvenience in order to have some time at home.

Blue Line transferred me to other tugs so that men could have some relief. I spent short periods on the *Seneca*, *Republic #5*, and the *John E. Matton*. Once when my tug was overhauling,

I went captain for a few weeks on the *Celtic* for McCarren Brothers. Another time I went aboard the *John J. Tucker*, which was chartered to Moran, and had only two men in the wheelhouse. I agreed to relieve each of them for one week so they could have some time home. The *Tucker* was an old wooden tug with 450 hp diesel. She did not have much power but she was heavy and had a big rudder. An extra pilot house had been added atop the old one so visibility was very good. If started back with care, she could be steered somewhat in reverse. It was customary to call Moran's dispatcher about 5 or 5:30 a.m. I would ask him for a shifting job and would generally get it. That type of work was enjoyed by me, but hated by my opposites. I guess we did well at shifting, because the dispatcher said that Bush Docks in Brooklyn requested us. It was busy work but the time passed quickly.

Republic # 5

Chapter 14

St. Joseph **with Blue Line # 1, Gulfport, Staten Island, N.Y., 1946**

The *Saint Joseph* was the next tug that entered my life. She remains as one of my all time favorites, though I can't explain why. The years I spent on the "Joe" were a time of hard work under great pressure yet I remember the ship with affection.

Blue Line purchased the oil barges of Valentine Oil Corp. and also their contracts so they would now be making oil deliveries to many more terminals in New York Harbor. A tug was needed that was low enough to go up the Harlem River and under the bridges without opening them, shallow enough for tide work in places like Eastchester Creek, and able to work in Newtown Creek. The *Saint Joseph* was selected to answer that need.

Purchased in Virginia, the tug was brought north and put in Perth Amboy Dry Dock for conversion to Blue Lines' needs. I was sent aboard as Master and to keep a check on the work. I was surprised to find that this was the old steamboat *Kevin Moran,* now converted to diesel, that had been built at Philadelphia, Pa.

in 1907. The hull was steel with deck and house of wood. The main deck, unpainted and scoured white, was immediately painted over. The brass running lights, hand rails and bitt tops were also painted. Deckhands would be busy enough without trying to maintain such frills. The large portholes of brass were not painted. Much polish and energy was expended to keep them shining but they did look great. The mast was replaced by a wooden mast that could be folded down when entering the Harlem River. The fo'csle was changed into a huge water tank. My daughter has the porthole that was removed with the companionway to the fo'csle.

Living quarters were good. The Master had a room in the rear of the pilot house equipped with lavatory and running water. The Mate had a room to himself on the main deck forward; engineers, deckhands, and cook and oiler were two to a room; galley was forward, in back of the Mate's and deckhands' rooms. The crew deserved the decent quarters and the new innerspring mattresses I got for them. They worked hard on that tug without complaining.

Our new oil contracts were to take us far up a foul, polluted body of water called Newtown Creek in Brooklyn. This smelly place would cause all brass to turn various shades of purple, ordinary white paint would turn yellow, and silver coins in ones pocket would become stained with brown. The acids and other pollutants in this water would eat the copper tubes out of the heat exchangers on the diesel engines after only a few trips in the creek. The *Saint Joseph* was fitted with a large water tank forward and another one aft. When the tug entered Newtown Creek the seacock was closed and the water from these tanks was circulated through the engines for cooling. This water, in turn, was cooled by being in contact with the metal hull and the sea water outside of it. The system worked very well. We were able to go far up the creek to Preferred Oil, above the Grand Street bridge, at low water. That was really smelly! Our prop would kick up chunks of material from the bottom that would float momentarily and it would look like blue smoke was coming from them. One of our engineers always got sick at these times.

The installation of the water tanks made it necessary to install smaller fuel tanks. As a result we carried only seven days fuel. We were so much in demand that it was hard to get the dispatcher to allow us time to refuel. The engineers were generally frantic after the sixth day. I would tell the dispatcher that this was my last request for fuel and if we ran dry he would be directly responsible for whatever happened. That would get results. I don't think the Coast Guard would have agreed that he was responsible. If running out of fuel caused an accident they would have hung me. The fuel dock we used most of the time was in the East River at Green point, Brooklyn, next to Liberty Dry Dock. The attendant would hand the hose to the oiler before we were tied up and fueling started immediately. In a short time we would be on our way. That was by far the fastest service I ever received at any oil dock. The same difficulty was encountered trying to find time to get a newspaper, replenish our freshwater supply, or to "grub up." Many times the cook was dropped off to get his provisions and then picked up again later. This was hard on the cook and made more work for the rest of us.

The easy relaxed days with Blue Line were gone forever. All of their tugs were busy and the *Saint Joseph* was the busiest. She was too much in demand. All Newtown Creek work was to be done by her because she was fitted out for it. When a barge went into the Harlem River the *St. Joe* got the job if she was available because she did not have to open the bridges. The oil barges that went into Eastchester Creek to Mount Vernon, N.Y. were also given to us whenever possible. There is a seven foot range of tide there and boats had to go in on the rising tide and get out before the tide fell too low. It was a very busy place and there would be a parade of sand scows, oil barges, and small tankers going in and out on each high tide. Each one wanted to get in and get some of the cargo off before the falling tide caused them to sit on the bottom. The channel was narrow, shallow, and crooked. A traffic bridge and a close-by railroad bridge crossed the mouth of the creek. They were narrow and not in line with one another, and the tide did not run straight through the piers. A tug with a barge alongside came in with a pretty good tide running diagonally across the draw of the traffic bridge which usually opened without delay. The barge was entered into the draw, the tug released from the barge to drop behind until through the bridge. The railroad bridge was very close and the barge was again picked up alongside and maneuvered to line up for the draw of the railroad bridge. The tug could fit through alongside in this bridge except with the largest barges. Very often this bridge would not open right away and this would cause some cussing and scrambling. The *Saint Joseph*, being a good handling tug of shallow draft, was ideal for this work. The dispatchers had to set their priorities as to where they would send us. It seems that we were always rushing to make some tide and were always a little bit late. We were constantly changing tows with the other tugs. They would start the loaded barges out for us because we just could not keep up. Our radiophone could not be shut off as we were being called constantly. We worked under constant pressure.

Once or twice a year we were given a barge load of heavy oil for delivery to one of the brickyards at Kingston. These were tide jobs and again the *Saint Joseph*, being handy and of shallow draft, was ideal for the job. What a treat to sail up and down the Hudson River in peace and quiet! Also, what a pleasure to wait for the barge while it pumped out. We appreciated these trips after the rat race we were involved in around the harbor. Some of the men sailing our tugs smoothly down the Sound used to wonder how we could stand to work like that.

Our greatest help came from the DPC #98, a Defense Plant Corporation tug that Blue Line had obtained from the Government. She was just as busy as we were and much of her work was taking up the slack for us when we fell behind.

The Defense Plant Corp. tugs were built during World War II to remedy the shortage of harbor tugs. They had a good design and many good features but also many drawbacks. All steel construction, a high pilot house, shallow draft, and good quarters, were all assets. A storage space in the bow was accessible from the galley and contained a large deep-freeze unit, the first I every saw on a tugboat. This storage area also contained a complete inventory of all spare parts for the engine. All portholes were equipped with blackout curtains. Pilot house controls, a good Sperry steering gear, and an electric capstan to pull hawser, were on the plus side.

The main engine was a 700 hp General Motors V-8 diesel such as was used in railroad locomotives. This was not great power but was adequate and gave them good speed running light. Two diesel-powered generators provided plenty of 110 DC electricity.

When listing the bad points, the first thing that comes to mind is the extreme discomfort from cold in winter weather. No insulation was used in these ships except for a few crumbs of cork placed in the paint on the interior of the steel house. This helped not at all. On top of this, the hot water heating system must have been figured out by an engineer using a formula for a well-insulated house. Each stateroom had a small convector type radiator which could not heat the room in very cold weather. The galley had a large convector type radiator fastened horizontally on the overhead directly above the galley table. It was located in the wrong place and provided no circulation of warm air. This did not matter because the oil-burning galley range was always running and produced plenty of heat. The pilot house had only a small radiator on the after bulkhead and was the coldest spot on the ship. Sheepskin coats and warm gloves were standard apparel there in the winter time.

A minimum of copper and brass was used in these ships because of the wartime shortage. The faucets were of unplated cast iron and the fog bell was cast from some iron alloy and had a poor tone.

Rudder power was not all that it could be. This, coupled with the shallow draft, made it more difficult to control heavy barges alongside. It was even more difficult to turn with a large light barge alongside when a breeze was blowing. After the war these tugs were sold to private industry and the purchaser usually installed pipe radiators under the pilothouse windows as should have been done originally. A great improvement in rudder power was obtained by adding cheek pieces to the rudders.

When the DPC tugs were built they were turned over to

towboat companies to use in their business. As I understood it, the Government agency paid each company a fixed amount each day for operating the tug. The government paid for all expenses, including wages, and kept all the revenue from the work done by each vessel. This meant that the company could not incur a loss from its operation but also could not reap tremendous profits. At the end of the war these tugs were sold individually to the company submitting the highest sealed bid. The one that had been operated by Blue Line was in good shape and they wanted to buy her at a reasonable price. I heard that some false information was allowed to leak out that she had a bent tail shaft and would require some expensive repairs. Whether or not this was true or had any effect on the price is not known by me, but the tug was purchased and named *Salutation*. The big steam tug of that name had been disposed of. Blue Line also bought two more of the DPC tugs and named them *Skipper* and *Seabee*.

One problem encountered on the *Saint Joseph* was the frequent breaking of the rudder cables. The steam steering engine had been converted to operate with compressed air. Each cable ran from the engine, around a sheave in the side of the house, through a pipe on deck, to a sheave on the stern deck, to the quadrant atop the rudder post. The sheaves were rather small so the cables made a sharp turn around them and after many flexings the cable would snap. The first break came after only about seven days operation. Riggers in the shipyard installed more flexible cables with a slight improvement. We broke the cables several times including once in Hell Gate. I had put some emergency tackle on the stern and we soon became adept at quickly hooking this up to the quadrant and maneuvering the tug in some dock. We never got into trouble from this but we had some excitement. After some experimenting it was found that a multi-strand cable of bronze worked quite well. It was very flexible and the constant bending around the sheaves did not break the strands. This would last up to a year without breaking. Each time the cables were replaced the deckhands would use the old ones to hang fenders.

Once when the cables were being changed at the shipyard the riggers said they had orders to take the old cables off with them. I said we needed them and would keep them, which we did. While I was taking my afternoon nap Blue Line's man in the yard, whose title might have been Marine Superintendent or Port Engineer, came down to the tug and made the deckhand give the old cables to the riggers. When I awoke and was told what had happened, I went to the riggers and got the cables back. I don't know why this man wanted the old coils of wire. Perhaps, being bronze, they had a scrap value. I had already had a couple of serious differences of opinion with him and we had gone to Bill Garrett to settle the matters. The judgment had been in my favor each time which I thought was proper because this man had never been aboard a tug before taking the job. He had no practical knowledge of tugboat operation. Charlie Quarry, the Master of the steam tug *Spartan*, had expressed his opinion of this man by telling him "I could handle your job but you sure as hell could not handle mine."

One Saturday morning a couple of weeks later, I was told to bring the tug into Pier #1 North River and come up to the office. Knowing something was amiss I went up to the office and found Bill Garrett there all alone, or so I thought. We exchanged pleasantries and then in walked the chief executive officer of the company, a man I had always thought of as cold, rude, and uninterested in the men on the boats. Garrett began questioning me about the cables and then I knew who was trying to get me into trouble. My explanation about fenders for the tug did not seem to make any impression but I had not shown my ace in the hole as yet. Blue Line had three small, ancient, wooden, lightships that were used as stakeboats. They were anchored, one each, at Bridgeport, Whitestone, and off Ellis Island. The office was on the top floor of Number One Broadway and had a fine view of the harbor. I suggested that the binoculars be used to inspect the Ellis Island Stake Boat. No fenders had been on this old relic before but now there were truck tires hanging on each side and on the stern. These protected the anchored boat, as well as the barge tied to her, from damage. All the tires, old wire cable, and old cable clamps, had been provided by me for the stake boat captain to hang these fenders. I knew that I was off the hook when the CEO turned and walked out. Garrett asked how much cable I had left and I said a six foot piece. He told me that the light coal barge on the stake boat was going to the shipyard for repairs and I should give the piece of wire to the bargeman for delivery to the man in the yard. I did not get a reprimand and was never questioned again about the old cables.

There was one group of tugboat workers that had it easy in wartime New York Harbor. Small diesel tugs had been built for the U.S. Army and these, plus some chartered tugs, were used for shifting around some of the piers. They were operated by civilian crews. Six or eight of these vessels would be used where normally one or two would suffice. They would go in rotation to make a short shift and then would kill as much time as possible so that one or more of the other tugs would get back to the dispatching spot before them. Then came a period of hanging on the end of the pier waiting to be called again. As a rough estimate, I would say that they worked three hours out of eight. This is what happens when bureaucracy gets involved in work that can be done better and cheaper by private industry.

I was Master of the *Saint Joseph* when "Victory in Europe" was proclaimed. It was a great day. The President asked all workers to stay on the job and a four day celebration could be held on V-J Day. When that day arrived the tug was in Perth Amboy Dry Dock for annual overhaul. Most of us in the crew were in a movie theater. An announcement was flashed on the screen that the war was over. We left the movie house and came upon a street full of wild celebrants. People were shouting, singing, dancing, and generally acting crazy. Impromptu parades of cars and people were going up and down Smith Street. Car horns were blaring on all sides. I don't remember seeing any of our feminine military personnel, but men in uniform were lionized. Women and girls were kissing every military man in sight. Others were carrying bottles and offering drinks to every uniform on the street. Some crewman from a Socony tanker that was in the shipyard went aboard ship to get their khakis. They hoped to be mistaken for Navy men. After watching the festivities for a time, my crew and I took off for our homes and returned four days later. Blue Line was a good outfit. They did not dock our pay for the four days off.

A New problem developed that had not been anticipated. Chemicals in the water of Newtown Creek had attacked the old steel hull and it had deteriorated badly. The tug was put into the shipyard and new steel doubler plates were welded to all of the hull below the water line. One of the welders used to tease me about my ship. When she was converted to diesel, concrete had been put in her bilges for stability, ballast, or some other reason. When installing a doubler plate on her bottom the worker experienced difficulty in welding the plate to the old hull. He found that he had been trying to weld the new plate to the smooth concrete under a thin spot in the hull. The nickname "Old Concrete Bottom" was suggested for the tug but happily it did not catch on.

Another problem began to plague us. We had frequent smokestack fires. Blue Line had been getting new diesels and promoting engineers. Several times our Chief had been put on a new tug and the assistants promoted. Each time we had a change in Chiefs the engine worked less hard and perhaps the lube oil was increased. The engine exhaust was not clean and the carbon and oil build-up would catch fire and burn with lots of flame and smoke. Our principal concerns were that the deckhouse did not catch fire where the exhaust went through, and that the sparks did not fall onto an oil barge or other flammable material. These fires became routine for us but were rather spectacular for others. Deckhands did not enjoy the constant scraping and repainting of the outer stack.

As the engine speed was reduced we found it more and more difficult to keep up. We no longer could do the same work as before. Some of the 20,000 bbl. barges had been put into heavy oil. When they were loaded decks-to, it was a struggle for us to handle them. It was obvious that the little Joe must soon be replaced by more horsepower.

There once was a time when we were mistaken for a larger ship. We came in off Long Island Sound with a light oil barge. When at Execution Rocks, with night falling, the fog came rolling in. By slowly groping our way, we managed to get to City Island and I had the bargeman drop his anchor. The splash of the anchor and the roar of the chain going out was very loud in the dense fog. Almost immediately the fog was lighted up by a light flashing AA, AA, AA. I had been able to read Morse code since my Boy Scout days so I sent back a T with the search light. I then received this message, "What is your name and port of registry?" I sent back "Saint Joseph" of Norfolk Va." Another question, "Do you need a pilot?" Answer, "Negative." Imagine the surprise at the pilot station when the fog cleared in the morning and their visitor turned out to be a little harbor tug.

Hudson River, July 4, 1946

I had some good men with me on that ship. John "Duke" Kern of Troy was my deckhand for over twenty years. Gene Ellis was my deckhand until he was drafted. Pete Negrich of Connecticut was my deckhand and later my Mate. Marty Negrich, his cousin, was my deckhand and later Mate on other tugs. Clayt Godfrey was Mate for more than a year before he went to Burlington, Vt. to finish his career on the ferryboats. Albert "Red" Acheson of Jersey City came to me as Mate from the old S & H steam tugs in the harbor. We became good friends and Red went on to eventually become Master of Blue Line's newest, biggest, and best diesel tug, the *Spartan*. "Ace" Gritmon of Newburgh was also my Mate. He was a very capable man and when the *Saratoga* was purchased he went aboard as Master. The *Saint Joseph* had some good men and a happy crew.

"Duke" Kern of Troy, N.Y. Author's deckhand for more than 20 years.

Saratoga

Chapter 15

The *Saratoga* was an 85 foot all steel tug built during World War II for the War Shipping Administration. Blue Line had purchased this vessel as an addition to the harbor fleet. When the *Saint Joseph* was sold my crew and I transferred to the *Saratoga*. Ace Gritmon, her Master, again became my First Mate or Alternate Master. This caused no trouble between us as we got on very well together. Ace was about the age of my father and had many years of experience. He was a clean living, capable man and a good shipmate.

Sleeping quarters were very good with only one or two men to a room. A comfortable space for the Master was in the rear of the pilot house. Staterooms on the main deck were equipped with one piece, watertight, doors. These were fine in a storm when they could be dogged down tight to keep seawater out. They were a nuisance the rest of the time because they were heavy and awkward to use. Half door would have been easier to handle and the bottom half could be closed while the top half could be left open for ventilation.

We were not enthusiastic about the main engine which had some problems but the increase in horsepower over our last tug made it easier to do the heavier work. She was also much more seaworthy and better fitted for work on Long Island Sound. There was no longer a problem with rudder cables breaking but we had something similar. The steering gear, a wartime design of the Montgomery Elevator Co., was unreliable. One never knew when it might suddenly stop working. The engineers became so used to it that they would usually have it working again in a few minutes. Sometime later, after I had left the tug, the company had a new Sperry gear installed.

The U.S. Army Transportation Corps had many vessels of this type. They were classified as harbor tugs and named ST (for small tug) followed by a number. To anyone interested I recommend *The Ordeal of Convoy NY 119* by Charles Dana Gibson II, published by South Street Museum of New York. It is the tale of a convoy which crossed the Atlantic in the fall of 1944. Included in the group were fourteen STs. Three of these small tugs, and 19 men from them, were lost at sea.

With the *Saint Joseph* gone, the *Saratoga* was now Blue Line's first choice for harbor jobs but we occasionally got out of town. Bigger barges were being sent into Eastchester Creek so we got ratchets and cables such as were used in the canal and pushed the loaded barges in. This was much easier than dropping them through the bridges. We did the Kingston brickyards and got to do more of the work on Long Island Sound. We were busy but did not have the great pressure on us as before.

I heard of a job nearer my home and with more time off, so I decided to leave Blue Line, although I was number 3 man on the pilot house seniority list. I was sure of a job as long as they had one tug in operation, but after the change, I would be at the bottom of the list. I phoned Bill Garrett and told him I was leaving. He wished me luck and said there would always be a job for me with Blue Line anytime I wanted it. That statement made me feel good.

The *Saratoga* was a comfortable ship with a good crew and a good boss, but I left her with no regrets. It did seem like the end of an era. When I started with the company, nine years before, they had four large steam tugs and one diesel, the *Seneca*. Now, when I left, they still had the *Seneca* plus six more diesels. The steamboats were gone.

Chapter 16

One sunny Sunday morning in December 1949, I towed the oil barge LTC # 38 to Port Newark. The bargeman, Harold "Red" Leeman of Maine, said that his company needed a pilothouse man for a tug operating between Rensselaer and Lake Champlain. He said it was a good job because the tug tied up almost every night. That sounded good to me. Red gave me the home phone number of the personnel man and I called and applied for the job. He said that he wanted a man for Lake Champlain, not a harbor man. I told him I was a licensed pilot for those waters. He said that a man familiar with Long Island Sound was needed because they ran to New Haven and Hartford in the winter. I replied that I was licensed for The Sound also. His last stipulation was that the tug also would run the Passaic River to East Rutherford, Eastchester Creek to Mount Vernon, and Jamaica Bay to Inwood, all difficult tide jobs. My answer was that I was accustomed to all three routes and had brought their barge LTC # 38 out of Inwood the night before. This brought the statement that the job was mine. I told him that I would complete my two week tour where I was and would be available after New Years Day. This was agreed to and so began my 22 year association with the tug *Canal Cities*.

I went aboard ship Jan. 3, 1950 and was told that I was to be 1st Mate or Alternate Master rather than 2nd Mate. That was okay with me as it was a little more money and meant that I would have to go on watch at midnight only one week instead of two on each tour of duty. The crew said they had been kept aboard on Christmas Day so the first time I called the office I told them I was giving them 12 months notice that I would not work on that holiday. This attitude and action from a new man is not recommended and might lead to dismissal, but they took no offense. The tug never worked another Christmas.

With canal pilot house 1950.

The *Canal Cities* had been built at Neponset, Massachu-
setts in 1943 for the Defense Plant Corp., a wartime government
agency, and named DPC 19. She was owned by Lake Tankers
Corporation whose name later was changed to National Marine
Service and was used in the movement of petroleum products for
Shell Oil Co. She was one of the Defense Plant Corporation tugs
built during the war such as Blue Line had obtained. The high
pilot house had been changed to be removable and was bolted on
in the Fall and removed in the Spring. For canal operation a small
wheelhouse was installed on the bow deck. The high house was
in place when I went aboard and it had the usual dinky little
radiator on the after bulkhead. Two portable heaters were used to
keep the pilots warm. The pilothouse controls for the engine were
a change for me after years of bell ringing. The control stand soon
became my favorite place to sit when on watch. At first, it seemed

strange to see the engineer walking around on deck with a cup of coffee while the tug was being maneuvered back and forth. I envied them. They had a great job, very little work to do, and an oiler to do it for them.

I had left a job as captain with high seniority to take a position as 2nd Mate with no seniority because the work was supposed to be easier. Now I found that the *Canal Cities* was to work for Blue Line throughout the winter, and we were to take our orders from them. I was on a different tug with a different company, but doing the same work! There were times in the next two weeks when I thought that the change had been a mistake. One night, after supper, the crew was all gathered in the galley except for the Captain who was steering the light tug up Newark Bay. The tug slowed down, stopped for a while, then went ahead and astern a couple of times, and

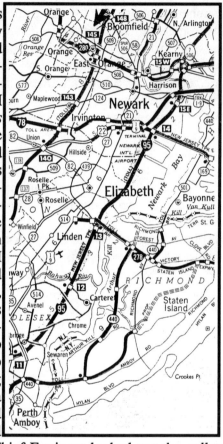

then went on again. The Chief Engineer looked out the galley door, said the captain ran aground, and calmly closed the door and resumed the conversation. It was bad enough that the tug was allowed to stray out of a well-marked channel, but the fact that the crew accepted it as a routine occurrence amazed me. The second week aboard was no better. The 2nd Mate had picked up the Blue Line #106 alongside and was bound up Arthur Kill. The barge had a full load of #6 oil and was deep in the water.

About 0100, when going through the draw of the B & O bridge at Elizabethport, the tug crashed into the wooden rack that protected the bridge pier. The heavy laden barge kept right on going breaking all the lines from the tug. I got out of bed and watched the mate pick the barge up again alongside. When things were again under control, I went back to bed. He headed the vessels up Newark Bay and in going through the draw of the Jersey Central RR bridge across the lower end of the bay, he crashed into the bridge abutment. The tug was again wiped off the barge breaking all lines, while the barge continued up the bay. When I entered the wheelhouse the mate was quite excited and shaken up so I took over and again picked up the barge. The deckhand was furious. Lines were being broken faster than he could splice them. Having calmed down, the mate again took over the wheel. He complained bitterly that the company should provide better decklines for us. My unspoken thought was that a rope that could withstand such treatment would be hard to find. Both bridges submitted claims for damages, but the tug was unharmed. I also noticed that, when towing the LTC #38, any time the ship's horn was used as a passing signal, the bargemen immediately came on deck to check it out. If they were afraid to sleep, there must be some reason for it. My own slumber was not as restful as it could have been.

It was a surprise when I found that the captain and mate were not familiar with the places the personnel man had questioned me about. They were constantly asking for pilots to take them into such places as Inwood and East Rutherford. I told them not to bother the office with these requests. No matter what watch it came on, I did the piloting and they soon were able to do it for themselves. My thoughts were that perhaps it had not been a very smart move when I changed jobs.

The *Canal Cities* had been working in a very relaxed manner, and the crew was not accustomed to the type of work we were now doing. They complained vociferously about the fact that the tug never stopped. Loud were the wailings on board, and many disgruntled reports went to Lake Tankers. I had no problem with the work. In fact, there was one very slight improvement.

We had no marine radiophone at this time, but were equipped with a mobile telephone like those used in automobiles. This meant that I no longer had to monitor the frequency all the time, but had only to answer when my phone rang. The FCC later had all of these phones removed from marine use and we had a different one installed. Great was the joy of the crew when we were sent to Oyster Bay for annual overhaul and the exchange of the wheelhouses preparatory to entering the Canal.

A barge was chartered for us to push and we loaded at Sewaren, N.J. for Rensselaer, then started our regular run to Burlington or Plattsburgh from Rensselaer or Sewaren. Once in a while we would get a trip to Utica, Syracuse, or Fultonville. After the spring high water season, we settled down to a relaxed canal season.

Result of hitting bridge.

Barge LTC # 38 at Sewaren, N.J. July 1964.
Hess Oil dock in background.

The Champlain division of the canal system was not as popular with the boatmen as was the Erie. It was not as deep, not as wide, had lower bridges, and the locks were more difficult to get into. There was no longer any freight on Lake Champlain except oil products. This tonnage had increased because of the jet fuel being hauled to Port Douglas for the U.S. Air Force. Because there had always been less traffic on the Champlain division, there were fewer pilots with local knowledge. The ones now working had refused to run Lake Champlain at night. This had been going on for years and now I was going to enjoy it. My enjoyment lasted only two or three months. The companies got together and issued an ultimatum to their men. All tugs would operate day and night at whatever speed was possible with safety, but they would not tie up. The men complied with the order, but there was some mumbling and grumbling.

After a thirteen year absence, the lake was still familiar to me. All of the old landmarks returned to mind. I was pleased to find that some dredging had been done in the marshes and that many new can and nun buoys had been added, plus some lighted buoys. The night time lake work bothered me not at all.

One of our deckhands, Russ Holland, whose father was a tugboat captain in Red Star, got his license and was made 2nd Mate. He was naturally a little nervous at first and complained to me that the captain always schemed to have the mate on watch at Lock #2 southbound, the most difficult lock. It was easy for me to understand because the same thing had been happening to me. I told him to do the work without complaining and not to try to counteract the scheming by doing the same thing. The crew was aware of what was going on and had no respect for their captain. About 90% of the time, the mates had this lock southbound. The following year the scheming was a little bit off schedule. The unit arrived at Lock #2 with a little water running at 1145 - fifteen minutes ahead of the planned time. No one sympathized with the captain when the barge lapped the bullnose and received extensive damage. Russ never had any trouble there. He became a very capable mate and was with us for a couple more years.

My father was master of the Burlington to Port Kent ferry boat *Valcour*. He bragged about how fast she was. When I suggested that my ship could provide some competition he pooh-poohed the idea which irked me more than a little bit. I told my chief engineer to pump out our water tanks and get ready to make a run. When the *Valcour* left Burlington ferry slip, we followed her out into the lake. Our speed allowed us to pass the ferry and then, as an added insult, cross her bow and return down the other side. My dad was upset by then and he always maintained that one of his engines was not working that day. My son was on the tug with me that day and got a big kick out of the boat race against his grandfather.

The summer went by very peacefully. On hot sunny days in the canal, the steel house would get very uncomfortable. A hose would be rigged to run water on the house to cool it somewhat. The men were clad only in cut off jeans or swim shorts and would cool off under the hose.

There were many nights in the autumn when we were forced to stop in the fog in the marshes. The deck lights illuminated the fog and the water around the tug. This in turn attracted many fish. A few of us were avid fisherman and welcomed this opportunity to fish while getting paid. We carried a supply of worms under the hawser rack and a tank of live bait in the lower engine room. The fishing was also very good at the ferry dock in Burlington. We never caught much fish at the Shell terminals at Burlington nor Plattsburgh. I now knew that I had made the right move when I changed jobs.

At the end of the pleasant canal season, we returned to New York and were sent to Oyster Bay to have the high pilot house bolted on. Everyone was pleased when our sister ship, the *Eastern Cities*, was put to work for Blue Line instead of us. That crew had been thoroughly spoiled with easy work and they also complained loudly about the change, but to no avail. We spent the winter running to New Haven and Hartford and supplying the terminals in the harbor area. The work kept us busy but we occasionally had some time off waiting for the barge to discharge cargo. It was a far better winter than the last.

In March 1951, the *Canal Cities* went to Oyster Bay and the high house was removed. The low wheelhouse had been remodeled and was now installed on the bow deck with a hydraulic ram under it. We now had an up and down retractable pilot house. The Cargill Grain Company had retractable houses on their grain barges and on the little tug *Carbany* in the canal, but this was the first tugboat doing canal and harbor work to be so equipped. We spent one day in Pier 1 North River demonstrating it and also gave many other showings. It was an instant success. The cost of changing wheelhouses each spring and fall was eliminated. Less water ballast was required in the barges when in the canal so our speed was increased and less time was lost discharging the ballast. The pilots formerly on the *Canal Cities* had, for several reasons, required seven days for a round trip from Rensselaer to Burlington and return. Now, because of the retractable house, we were making the trip in three days as regular as clockwork. Our record of making the fastest round trips in the Champlain Canal did not last long. Other companies built new,

Being fitted with retractable pilot house at Oyster Bay, N.Y. March 1950.

more powerful, tugs that were already equipped with the new pilot house and they surpassed us.

About a year later another improvement was made — radar was installed. We on the tug had not wanted it and had done what little we could to fight against it. What a mistake that was! The radar soon became our shipmate and best friend. It contributed greatly to safety and paid for itself many times over. The good radar is responsible for the reputation I had aboard ship as a "fog eater."

The *Canal Cities* had always rolled badly in any kind of a sea except dead ahead or dead astern. With the addition of so much weight so far forward, she was even worse. It didn't matter because we worked mostly in sheltered waters. The only times we went on the Great Lakes was when we made short trips on Lake Ontario, about twice a year, to Sackett's Harbor.

The office once asked me about making four trips to Philadelphia. I refused, saying the ship was not seaworthy for coastwise travel. Our new pilot house was a loose fit. If we took water over the bow in any amount it would get into our forward storage area. The plate on deck over the stern hatch could not be fastened down because the studs had been allowed to rust and nuts could not be turned on them. The doors on the deckhouse had warped and were no longer water tight. A man came down from the office to look us over and he wanted no help from the crew, which is what he received. His solution was very simple. Hand rails were welded to the house on each side. Now the men had something to hold onto in a sea and the ship was now seaworthy. So much for the amount of practical experience held by our superiors.

We were sent to Providence, R.I. and to Boston, but we kept a close watch on the weather. Storms on Lake Champlain could not harm us but they did make us uncomfortable a few times. We took water inside the ship, but never in any amount to be dangerous.

One night, I left Burlington with the chartered barge on the sea hawser. It had been a split load; half had been discharged at Burlington and the balance was to go to Plattsburgh. The wind was blowing hard from the south, creating a beam sea for us crossing the lake. The tug rolled horribly. I dropped the wheelhouse all the way down but we still rolled very badly and the house clattered back and forth within its steel shell. The men on the port side could not get out of their rooms. There was no sense in continuing in that fashion so I headed south. Immediately the rolling changed to pitching which we could handle. We buried the stem head each time we went into a sea but the waves were getting smaller with each mile traveled south. After we passed Four Brothers Islands, I circled around and headed north on the West side of them. We now carried the stern sea past Schuyler Island and then headed up behind Valcour Island. This put us in the lee of Trembleu Mountain and the sea was reduced to a chop. The dock man at Plattsburgh wondered what took us so long to cross the lake.

Another time the barge was pumping out at Plattsburgh when the wind began to freshen up from the southeast. The barge began bouncing and banging against the dock but managed to pump out all the cargo. All docklines were taken in and the mate took the barge away from the dock on a single stern line. They were well off the dock, putting out the sea hawser, when somehow they backed over the line and picked it up in the propeller. The tug was now helpless. The bargeman threw our line off his bow and dropped his anchor which held him safely. We had a small Danforth anchor on our bow and we threw it over tied to a headline, but it could not hold us. With every surge of the sea the little anchor dragged. Our captain had placed the ship's anchor under the hawser rack and bolted it to the deck. By the time fastenings were broken loose from the rust and paint, the tug had been blown ashore. She was stranded parallel to the shore, and every wave raised the tug and banged her on the bottom. The marine radiophone was of no use to us because there was no shore station we could reach and tugs did not monitor any frequency on Lake Champlain. Someone had to get ashore to a phone. We launched our lifeboat and my deckhand and I put the Mate and his deckhand ashore. They got their feet wet, but we two with the lifeboat got wet up to our armpits keeping the craft from crashing ashore in the surf. I told the Mate to go up to the New York State Police and ask them to come down with their boat and assist us. The police yacht arrived just after daybreak. After a couple of tries, they had us afloat again. We were taken behind the break-water and tied up to the railroad dock. Now that we were safely tied up, I inquired about getting a diver. A member of the Plattsburgh Fire Department was a hard hat diver and I hired him to come down and help us. When it was time for the New York office to be open, I called the boss, gave him a complete report, and had my actions approved. By afternoon the diver had the rope cut away and we were ready to leave. I paid him and also gave the two troopers a substantial expression of our gratitude. Their yacht had been damaged slightly. Having no towing bitts, they had put a timber across two seats to fasten the line to. One seat back had been broken when towing us. They did a fine job. We got underway after a loss of about 15 hours. Our propeller had been damaged and we limped along until we could get to a shipyard. The tug's bottom was dented and that winter it was cut away and replaced by heavier steel plates. The big boss came on board and approved my expenditures even though I naturally could produce no receipt for some of them. He complimented me on my handling of the situation.

After a few years went by, National Marine Service (they had changed the name) closed the New York office. All of their marine equipment was sold except the tug *Canal Cities* and the barge LTC #38. Our office force was now in Perth Amboy and consisted of one man, Charles LeMoon, who had been Chief Engineer of their tanker *Lake Charles.*

There were only three tugboat pilot jobs and I was number four. The captain of the *Eastern Cities* came over as Master. The office offered the captain of the *Canal Cities* a cash settlement if he would retire early. When he accepted the offer there was now room for me and I was kept on as alternate master.

Our summer work was changing. We no longer went to Utica nor Syracuse. Those plants were now on a pipe line. The terminal at Fultonville changed owners so we no longer went there. The trips to Burlington and Plattsburgh kept us busy for awhile in the Spring and again in the Fall. In between these times, we worked in New York with an occasional trip up the Hudson to Milton.

One morning when going into Eastchester Creek, the captain had a heart attack and was sent to a hospital in an ambulance. He never returned. I was promoted to master, a position I held until the fall of 1971.

Parts of two winters were spent working in Hudson River ice. We lacked the horsepower needed for this work. Many times the Coast Guard ice breakers came to our assistance and towed us through the heavy spots. One of them wanted to put a hawser on my bow. I refused it because I was towing a loaded barge on stern lines. I did not want to be rolled upside down as had happened before, to another tug, with such a maneuver. He finally put his hawser on the bow of the barge and I got behind it. That was much safer.

Once I asked for help and didn't get it. We were southbound with a light barge on sternlines and we got stuck near Storm King Mountain. The floating ice always packed in that area and especially at West Point. We could not move and the ebb tide was packing more ice around us. The tug was listed far over and chunks of ice were being forced right over our rails and onto the deck. A Coast Guard cutter, I think it was the *Mahoning*, was tied up at Newburgh so I called on the radio, explained our situation, and asked for help. The skipper said it was after 1600 hours, they were tired, but would be out at 0800 tomorrow. I was shocked that they would not come to our assistance. We put a ladder from our stern deck to the bow of the barge as an escape route in case we capsized. The next few hours were spent throwing chunks of ice off the deck on the low side and watching to see if we were going to come back upright. Finally the tide changed to flood and the loose ice began drifting north. We again began trying to get through and after several hours were successful. When the little ice breaker came out at 0800 we were gone. He probably thought that this supported his decision not to come to our aid. His ears should have burned from the comments made about him by my crew during the two or three critical hours of the night.

U.S. Coast Guard cutter *Manitou*, Storm King Mt. Jan. 2, 1956.

I met another Coast Guard officer who impressed me with his skill and knowledge. He was in command of the flower class vessel *Mariposa*. This vessel had assisted us several times, always with courtesy and efficiency. On this trip, I was bound for Milton with a loaded barge and the *Mariposa* came along. We were almost to our destination. I asked him to break a channel in to the dock for me as he went past, and it was done. After the barge was tied up, I took the light tug to Poughkeepsie and tied up alongside the *Mariposa* which had stopped there for the night. A sailor came over and said that his skipper invited me over to the wardroom for a cup of coffee. I was glad to accept the invitation. We had some coffee and some good conversation. During this talk my information on the type of vessel was updated. I had thought they were sea-going vessels built to service lighthouses and buoys along the coast, and were used to break ice only when regular ice breakers were not available. The skipper told me that this class of vessel was built with ice breaking capability, having a rein-forced hull, steel propeller, and a specially designed stem. He told an ensign to get the blueprints out of the safe so he could show me this special stem. The ensign(replied that this was classified material and should not be shown to me. The skipper said to bring them out as there was no point in calling the material classified when several of the ships had been given to the Russians. The ensign complied with resentful glances toward me. He almost made me feel like a spy.

Once we lost a very good cook because of work in the ice. We were southbound with a light barge on short sternlines. It would have been better to push but we couldn't see over the barge and we couldn't get through the ice when alongside. The river was not tightly frozen but had stretches of open water and large fields of floating ice. When these floes were of thin ice, the tug would force its way through them followed by the barge. When the heavier floes were encountered it was a different story. The tug would be stopped by the ice and the barge would bang into the stern. The angle of the bow on the barge would force the tug's stern deeper in the water, thus raising the bow higher. This push would force the tug to break the ice and she would lunge ahead.

This would cause her to fetch up on one stern line before the other causing her to roll. Most times the ice would crack at an angle causing the tug to veer to one side. This required fast action from the pilot so that he stayed straight in front of the barge and did not get run over. Only a few seconds elapsed during this excitement. The pilot had to be alert at all times. Sleep was difficult for the crew. They needed to have confidence in the pilot house men to even go to bed. Apparently the cook did not have this confidence. He quit, saying that he was not paid enough for that hazardous duty.

One trip in the Hudson River ice was worse than all the others. We left Sewaren with the LTC #38 loaded, bound for Rensselaer. Traffic on the river, other than ships, had been traveling in convoys escorted by an ice breaker. Our office had not taken advantage of this service and we went up the river completely on our own. Progress could be made only by breaking out a channel with the light tug and then towing the barge through it. We could not push the barge through the ice even after a track had been broken. The broken ice piled up in front of the square bow of the barge and stopped our headway. By towing the barge on short sternlines, our propwash kicked the broken ice under and around the bow of the barge allowing us to make some very slow progress. Our engine overheated badly from the heavy load and slow speed through the water. When the throttle was pulled back somewhat, to keep the engine from overheating, our progress would stop. By allowing the engine to idle until cool and then running at normal speed as long as possible, we were able to travel short distances. This constant fluctuation in temperature certainly was doing the engine no good. Also, the close-up towing of the loaded barge and the propeller hitting cakes of ice was shaking the whole ship and putting great strain on the engine. The engineer was frantic. He told me we would have to shut down. I had reported our problems to the office and had been told to keep going as long as progress could be made. The engineer was invited to call the office and tell them he refused to run the engine any more, but he declined. The strength of the hull was also severely tested. Full speed with the light tug was required to break a path. Luckily we sustained no damage other than minor denting.

It took us four days to make the trip north. Two nights we shut down from midnight to 0600 so we could get some sleep. One night we were unable to move but a ship overtook us in the early morning and broke a track for us. On arrival at Albany, the First Assistant called the chief at home to come and relieve him. The assistant did not want to be responsible for the engine when working under such conditions. I could sympathize with him. The tug took a lot of abuse but seemed to suffer no permanent damage except for the propeller which was badly bent and needed to be changed. Compared to the trip up, the return with the light barge was uneventful.

Some people had predicted that the new pilot house would be knocked off by hitting a bridge. After many years of operation this prediction finally came true. A temporary second mate had been hired and he was not familiar with the up and down house. Early one morning, he failed to lower it far enough and it crashed into a bridge. He crouched down behind the steering wheel and was uninjured, but the pilot house was wrecked. The tug was taken to Matton's Shipyard at Cohoes to have a new house built and installed.

National Marine Service hired the tug *H.A. Meldrum* from Matton on a bare boat charter. The owner put Charlie Gibbs of Waterford on board as Chief Engineer and the *Canal Cities* crew took over. The *Meldrum* was an old diesel-powered wooden tug that had been converted from steam some years before. Living quarters were not as good as we had become accustomed to. The galley was smaller and not as well equipped. She was not pilot house controlled so the engineers had to stand watch in the engine room to answer bell signals. I was not thrilled with the return back to a low pilot house and no radar. It was not the ideal replacement vessel, but we were pleased that we kept our jobs while repairs were being made.

The *Meldrum* gave us one unforgettable experience that fall. We left Plattsburgh early one morning with the barge on hawser and headed down behind Valcour Island. The wind was picking up and it started to snow. Frank Egan of Kingston, a very capable man, was the mate on watch. He called me to the pilot house just before 0530. It was about time for me to get up and he wanted to show me the lights of Port Kent off the starboard. They were rapidly fading in the increasing snow and he wanted me to have some idea of our position. The water was not really rough but it was choppy enough to make the old wooden tug bounce around a bit. The First Assistant reported that we were in trouble because the hull was leaking badly. The engine was slowed down to relieve the stress on the hull. In a short time, he returned and said he could not stay ahead of the water coming in and we would soon sink. That gave me something to think about. The bargemen were asleep and I knew they would not hear the tug's horn.

H.A. Meldrum as a steamboat before conversion to diesel.

It was too windy and choppy to back up to the bow of the barge and hammer on it to awaken them. That meant we could not anchor the barge. Visibility in the heavy snow was down to about 200 feet. We had no radar and were not sure of our position.

I considered making a 90 degree turn to starboard and beaching the tug wherever we arrived at land. The problem with this was that we would probably run into Trembleu Mountain where the deep water was close to the shoreline. If the full length of the tug could not be placed on the bottom she would sink. There wa no lifeboat so the crew would get wet in getting ashore. The area was sparsely populated and it might be hours in the wind and cold before shelter could be found. I was just about to put this plan into operation when the Second Assistant came into the pilot house and said that since we slowed down the pumps were keeping up with the water coming in. The First Assistant was panicky and said we were sinking and the oiler was already wearing a life vest. I decided that the Second, being more in control of himself, had the better information so I stayed on course. Reports from the engine room at fifteen minute intervals proved that he was right.

We were not making much headway and our estimated position was a guess, at best. Fortunately, we made the course good. I got a brief glimpse of Schuyler Island and was

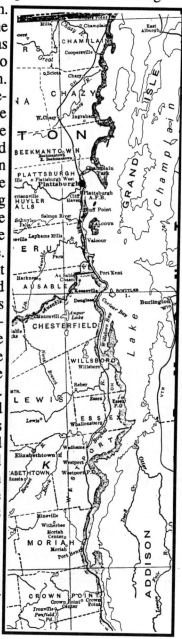

able to change course down the lake. By the time we arrived at the Four Brothers, visibility had improved and the lake had calmed down to a little chop. The bilge water was under control, the crew off watch had finally gone to bed, and the oiler had removed his life belt. The First was still nervous and it took some talking before he would increase the engine speed to about three fourths of normal. When this did not cause more leaking, I finally got him to run the engine "hooked up."

We were far behind schedule. It was change crew day and our relief was to meet us in Whitehall. I had called my wife to meet me at 2:00 p.m., it was after six when we finally arrived. The First Assistant was not much of a drinking man but he headed for the nearest bar to calm his nerves with alcohol. He was going on his week off so it was okay. I got into my car and drove home, very happy to be there, even if I was late.

When the tug was taken off charter, I told Ralph Matton about the leak. He said he knew about it, but had put the tug on dry dock and been unable to find it. He asked if his Chief Engineer, Charlie Gibbs, had been excited. I truthfully told him that it had not bothered Charlie at all. What I did not tell him was that Charlie, unknown to his boss, was taking his time off right along with the rest of the crew and was not aboard that morning.

We were all pleased to get back to our old home, the *Canal Cities*. This tugboat had the distinction of possibly being the only tugboat in the United States with an amateur radio station on board.

I operated WB2 GAL mobile from the tug for several years. The transceiver was 100 watts to a small verticle antenna atop the pilot house. This antenna was of the type used on automobiles and was mounted on a spring. A cord from the antenna leading into the pilot house allowed it to be pulled down to horizontal to go under the bridges. Because of the all steel vessel and the good ground, the signal from this station was very strong. I had many interesting chats with hams in the U.S. and in foreign countries, but the station I worked more than any other was K2 YJR in North Syracuse. My friend Ray, the operator, was very interested in tugboats and was also from my hometown.

Many times, when I was driving to or from work in my car, he kept me company via radio. The novelty of a ham station on a tugboat assured me of many contacts and I enjoyed them immensely.

My last years on the *Canal Cities* were spent mostly in New York harbor, but it was still a very good job because we usually waited for the oil barge to load and discharge cargo. I was driving my car back and forth to work, which was convenient. It seemed that I had come full circle. Having joined this vessel more than 21 years ago for an easier job away from the harbor, I was now right back in New York, but on a better job.

In september of 1971, while I was home on time off, I suffered a heart attack. Weeks later the boss called and told me that the company had ceased operations in New York and the *Canal Cities* had been sold. My answer was that it was too bad that the company had not been able to survive without me. That ended my long cruise on a ship that had treated me well and left me with many fond memories.

Entering Lock # 2C with LTC # 38.

Chapter 17

At Lock # 7, Fort Edward with pilot house fully retracted.

Early in 1972, I telephone Martin Kehoe to ask if any jobs were available. My reasons for this were two fold; first, his tugs worked mostly in the Champlain Canal which was near my home; second, the chance of being hired was better with a small company than with a large one. After a few minutes conversation, I was hired as master of the *Colleen Kehoe*, which was tied up but would be brought out when the Champlain Canal opened.

The *Colleen Kehoe* was an all steel tug with a 450 hp Fairbanks Morse diesel. Built by Ira Bushey, Inc. in Brooklyn, N.Y. in 1936 as the *Choctaw*, she was one of many of this type. One great improvement had been made — a good, high, retractable pilot house had been added.

When the first few tugs of this series were built, they were classified as "power houses" in the canal. There had been no comparison between them and the tired old steamboats still operating. These new diesels had more power and produced more work at lower cost. They required no firemen and no licensed men; stops for fuel were much less frequent and as a bonus for the crew, they were much cleaner. Two stacks were on the upper deck; one concealed the exhaust pipe and the other was an air intake. Exhaust noise was very loud, but less noticeable aboard ship than away from it. When I lived on 1st Avenue in North Troy, these tugs would go past hooked up and rattle the windows of my house. One could always tell the Bushey Tugs by the noise.

Two of these tugs towed Hedger boxes in the 30's. The bargemen had complaints about them as being too strong and pulling out sheaves, etc.; not being able to run the engine dead slow, as with the steam tugs, caused more complaints. The tows entered the locks at greater speed and were thus harder to stop and subject to more damage if a mistake was made.

Now, forty years later, these tugs had the lowest horsepower in the canal and the horses were very tired. Time had exacted its toll and rust was eating them up. The up and down wheelhouses installed on some of them had greatly increased their value and probably extended their useful life.

The *Colleen Kehoe* was typical of these vessels. Her retractable house worked very well but there was no radar and not even a compass. Breakdowns of the weary old engine occurred frequently and spare parts were hard to find.

When these tugs were new, the deckhouses were grained to resemble wood paneling and made a very nice appearance. World War II caused them to be painted grey and after the war the color was not changed. Kehoe had the house grained again and the old girl looked fine. Like a good application of make-up on an old woman, this concealed her age and true condition. Rust had attacked the hull. In my room, a hole six inches across had been eaten through the steel deck allowing a good view of the lower engine room. I patched it with wire mesh and cement. Back in my steamboat days, I had worked on tugs in worse shape.

At canal opening time, we brought the tug out of Columbia St., Brooklyn, and picked up a loaded oil barge for the canal.

Most of the summer we ran to Burlington, Plattsburgh, Ticonderoga, with a couple of trips to Oswego. The barge we were towing had no batteries and ran a 110 volt dc generator 24 hours a day. This was great for us. We put 110 volt bulbs in our searchlights and used the power from the barge to light up the canal. A different barge was towed for a time and our old 32 volt dc generator could not give us an equal amount of light.

High water caused us to have one afternoon of excitement. Three Kehoe tugs with barges were tied up at Lock #4 for high water. Flood conditions had abated but the water was still above normal. Kehoe decided that it was time to get moving. The first two tugs were to help each other into Lock #2, which they did. One unit made it safely and the other suffered some small damage. My mate arrived in Lock #3 with the barge and then decided he would not go any farther. I relieved him and got underway. The strong current pushed our barge onto the boom along the piers on the east side of the river. We slid the full length of the boom with the port stern corner just touching the boom. A valiant effort was made, but the old girl did not have enough push to overcome the force of the current. The barge hit the hard rock at the end of the boom and cut a gash in the side near the stern.

Immediate flooding of the pump room occurred and the port stern corner of the barge became deeper and also caused a list to port. There was no way to stop so we continued on. The tug that was to help approached us above Lock #2 but parted his line and we went into the lock unassisted. We had no difficulty. I felt proud that we had successfully entered the lock without help, but I also felt bad about the damage to the barge.

As the season progressed, we had several breakdowns and I did not appreciate being laid off each time. Differences of opinion between the owner and me about the lack of a compass and other things caused me to feel it was time to move on. Early that fall I left to take another job. There were no regrets about leaving the *Colleen Kehoe.*

New York City, a busy port for years, has been even more active since the Erie Canal was built. Much of the produce of the West and North comes by way of the canal. It is re-shipped at New York to other coastal ports and all over the world. This is a view of South Street from Maiden Lane.

Chapter 18

Sheila Moran, **Utica Canal Terminal 1973**

In the fall of 1972, I took a job as Second Mate on the *Mohawk* of Moran Towing; a small, all steel, square ended, western style, towboat. Being all steel, shallow draft, twin screw, with pushing knees, one would think that this was the ideal vessel for pushing barges in the canal. I did not find it so. In my opinion she was too light and was under powered. When Lake Champlain became a little rough she would pound against the barge much worse than would a tug with its bow recessed into the V-shaped stern of the barge. It is common knowledge that this style of towboat is not meant to run in rough water. I never saw the *Mohawk* in real bad weather but I think she would fall off a lot with the wind and would not survive a bad storm.

I had read and heard tales of the western style towboats with their great pilot house equipment and their ability to maneuver heavy tows in almost any direction. Those vessels had lots of space, air conditioned rooms, laundry rooms, and rec rooms. This was not the case with the *Mohawk*. The rooms were not great and the galley was poorly designed with very little eating space. The steel house had insufficient insulation so she was hot in hot weather, cold in cold weather, and noisy all the time. This was not a vessel one would fall in love with.

The *Mohawk* was sold and Moran transferred Capt. Earl "Chip" Costello and his crew to the *Sheila Moran*.

Chip was the youngest of three brothers, originally from Waterford, who all became tugboat captains. Their father, Capt. Joe Costello, had been owner of the tug *Lloyd H. Dalzell*. In the 1920's this tug had operated as a day boat in the Waterford area and the older boys gained their tugboat experience at early ages. Capt. Joe had a license as pilot and a license as engineer. When he had a job for the tug he hired whichever man was available and he operated the other end. Chip left Moran a few years later and became Master of the NYS DPW tug *Governor Cleveland*.

The *Sheila Moran* was a good all steel tugboat but was just beginning to show her age. She was built at Beaumont, Texas in 1941. Her original low pilot house was later replaced by a retractable model which made her better equipped for work in the canal and also in the harbor. It seemed good to be back on a real tugboat after the few months spent on the steel box. Like all of the tugs built for the canal in recent years, she had a good retractable pilot house.

Much of the summer was spent in the canal towing oil to Utica and other places. During the slack spells we worked in New York doing whatever was asked of us. We occasionally worked on ships but this work was usually reserved for the harbor tugs. It annoyed me to enter the harbor after several days of steady running, and have the dispatcher give our barge to a local tug and hand us a mud scow to take to sea or some other such job. We would see tugs hanging on while we, who had been working steadily, were not given time to even get a newspaper. It seemed that the "short stackers" were not appreciated in the office. Moran had started in the canal and had built the company from the profits made there. I guess they were getting away from their roots.

Tugboats were no longer fun. Each time, when home, I was reluctant to return. Many years had been spent learning my trade and I felt that I was at my peak. From now on, it would be all down hill. I decided to seek my version of a snug harbor. At age 58 I retired from my long association with tugboats.

Sheila Moran **at Lock # 17, Little Falls, N.Y.**

Sheila Moran entering Lock # 17, Little Falls, N.Y.
Highest single lock in the New York State System.

Afterword

This discourse was meant to be about tugboats and I apologize if it seems to be more of an autobiography. My purpose was to record some of the details of the way of life aboard these small craft. I particularly wanted to tell of the old steam tugs before those of us who knew them are all gone. My experiences should not be considered as the norm for all who worked in those days. Other people, in other companies, would find things entirely different.

Many changes occurred to tugboats during my lifetime. They have evolved from the wooden, coal-fired, dirty, steamboats of few creature comforts, to the modern, all steel, powerful, tugboats of today. The cordage has changed from manila hemp to the stronger and lighter polys and nylon. Radio telephones and radar are now standard equipment. Accommodations for the crew are better and sanitary facilities much improved.

New York harbor is no longer the busy port it once was and commercial traffic on the canal system is almost nil. Steam powered tugboats no longer exist except in the memories of some of us old timers.

It is my hope that I have provided some knowledge and entertainment for you, the reader.

**Author with two good shipmates -
a cup of coffee and the radar stand it sits on.**

Index

Q

Quarry, Charlie, 99
Quick, Bob, 12 - 14, 16, 18, 41, 46 - 47

R

Red Star, 113
Reliance Marine Corp., 79 - 80
Rensselaer, N.Y., 81, 107, 111, 114, 121
Republic #5, 91 - 92
Richelieu River, 9, 42, 50
Robert H. Cook, 27, 30
Roberts, Bob, 13
Roberts, Harold, 13
Robin Hood, 86
Rochester, N.Y., 63, 80, 85
Rockland #1, 33
Rome, N.Y., 17, 81
Rondout Creek, 37, 57 - 58
Ross, Reginald, ii
Rouses Point, 42 - 43
Rouses Point Bridge, 42
Ryan, Bill, 59

S

Sachem, 73
Sackett's Harbor, 115
Saint Jean, P.Q., Canada, 9, 17, 25, 41 - 42, 49 - 50
Saint Joseph, 93 - 94, 98, 100, 105
Salutation, 90
Saratoga, 103 - 106
Schenectady, N.Y., 4, 55
Schuyler Island, 116, 124
Seabee, 98
Seaman's Church Institute, 84
Searles Ferry, 5, 13
Seneca, 91, 106
Sewaren, N.J., 111 - 112, 121
Shell Oil Co., 109
Shell Oil terminals, 114
Shiela Moran, 131 - 133
Shinvier, Charley, 36
Shithouse Bend, 53
Skipper, 98

Smith, Coleman, 20
Smith, George, 27 - 28, 35
Snake Den, 42
Socony #6, 79
Socony tankers, 46
South Amboy, N.J., 90
South Street Museum of N.Y. 106
Spartan, 73, 99, 103
Stamford, Ct., 90
Standard Oil, 20
Staten Island, 39, 41
Staten Island Ferry, 25
Staten Island, N.Y., 93
Stepping Stone Lighthouse, 90
Storm King Mountain, 118
"The Stumps", 50
Sulphur King, 63
Sun Oil, 83
Suprenant, Leo, 62
Sweeney, Capt., 30
Sweet, Bill, 20
Syracuse, N.Y., 111, 118, 125

T

Taft, Matt, 49
TenEyck, George, 5
Thomas A. Feeney, 79 - 80, 83, 88
Three River Point, 86
Throggs Neck , 88
Ticonderoga, N.Y., 129
toilet facilities, 3, 8
Tonawanda, N.Y., 16, 87
Tottenville, N.Y., 41
Trembleu Mountain, 116, 124
Triton, 1 - 4, 13, 19
Troy, N.Y., 10, 28, 35, 43, 49, 55, 59, 102

U

U.S. Coast Guard, 72, 75 - 77, 87, 89 - 90, 95, 118
U.S. Navy, 88
U.S. Transportation Corps, 105
Unions
    Licensed Tugmen's Protective